PHILOSOPHY IN THE MIDDLE AGES

PHILOSOPHY IN THE MIDDLE AGES

An Introduction

by Paul Vignaux

translated from the French by E. C. Hall

GREENWOOD PRESS, PUBLISHERS
WESTPORT, CONNECTICUT

The Library of Congress has catalogued this publication as follows:

Library of Congress Cataloging in Publication Data

Vignaux, Paul.
   Philosophy in the Middle Ages.

   Translated from the third French ed. with title:
Philosophie au moyen âge, which was originally published
under title: La pensée au moyen âge.
   Bibliography: p.
   1. Philosophy, Medieval. 2. Religious thought--
Middle Ages. I. Title.
[B721.V513 1973]   189   72-8244
ISBN 0-8371-6546-6

79697

CONTENTS

PHILOSOPHY IN THE MIDDLE AGES

INTRODUCTION

A few words of explanation would seem to be necessary at the beginning of this book in order to define its specific intention and to distinguish it from other works dealing with the same material.

Concerned only with the Latin West, the first and second editions of this book presented a brief history of medieval *thought* rather than of medieval *philosophy;* this last word was purposely avoided in earlier editions so as not to prejudge the philosophical character of medieval speculation. It is, in fact, precisely this characteristic that is often questioned along with the inclusion of the medieval period in the elaboration of a history of philosophy. It is merely to draw attention to this problem, and not to suppose that it has been resolved, that in the title of this, the third revised edition, the word "philosophy" appears.

Ideally the historian of philosophic doctrines attempts to recover the viewpoint of their authors; he tries to see their intellectual task as they saw it themselves; if possible, he seeks in their works a definition of what they hoped to achieve by formulating them. This exigency leads to treating medieval thought as theological when seen as a whole, since its speculation has reference to a "Revelation"—the source, both in the eyes of the believer and in itself, of concepts that are more than human. But it must also be pointed out that medieval men had rather varied conceptions of this theological way of thinking. The study of this variety —as yet scarcely begun—indicates that these conceptions have their origins in *philosophies* that preceded the Middle Ages as well as continuity with those that followed. But concerning "the philosophers" and the discipline they founded, medieval theologians had ideas of their own, which were not unrelated to those that they formulated regarding their own discipline, and which were as varied as their conceptions of theology. There are then apparently very diverse elements in the answer that the historian can give to the interlocutory question that gives this book its title: What place should be made in the history of philosophy for a typically theological age? It would be impossible to present a number of these elements, leaving the answer to the reader, without dispelling the still too common conception of the Middle Ages as possessed of an intellectual unity so great that the period is given an appearance of poverty. Above all else, it is the purpose of this study to convey to the reader a very contrary impression, which the author will try to prove: an impression of diversity.

How can this diversity be presented? In so few pages it is impossible to explain entire systems with even a minimum of detail and character. For the historian of thought, the theses which form a system are less interesting than the manner in which problems are posed and dealt with. Before anything else can be done, is it not necessary to define the medieval frame of reference and its method of procedure? Since it is not possible here to offer an exposition of the philosophical or theological systems of the Middle Ages, would it not be wiser to content oneself with describing and evoking the diversity of the individuals who expressed themselves in these works? This would be a relatively simple task and one that would not be devoid of a certain delight. But when one seeks to understand works of thought, is it legitimate to extract or to separate the inspiration from the body of doctrine it vitalizes and from the technical form in which it is expressed? Thinking is like a craft. Since we must study different modes of thought, we cannot neglect the technique or even the language itself. These brief remarks suffice, I think, to justify the examination of some rather abstract questions in this book, and the somewhat abundant use of quotations. In order to answer the needs of a larger public, the Latin passages are usually either preceded or followed by a more or less literal translation of the original text. Nevertheless the reader will find himself carried into a rather strange world. We will feel that we have betrayed the reality of the Middle Ages, the difference between that age and our own, if in following this exposition, our contemporaries do not find themselves bewildered by its theological matter and technical form. However, unless such obstacles can be surmounted, no one today can enter into the realm of medieval thought, or, for that matter, into the spirit of another civilization.

It is enough to be attentive to the technical form of works of thought in order to grasp the importance, sometimes misunderstood, of certain aspects of the intellectual life of the Middle Ages: the shaping of the mind by such closely related disciplines as grammar and logic; the use of dialectic, identified with reason itself, as a universal instrument of achieving knowledge; the fundamental character of the relationship of meaning between words (*voces*) and things (*res*) essential in the "nominalisms" of both the twelfth and the fourteenth centuries.

Beneath the abstract exterior of scholastic formulas and conventional Aristotelian language, one can nevertheless perceive the relevance that certain academic questions had for the lives of the men who discussed them. A remarkable example of such questions, and of the lively spirit in which they were discussed during the Middle Ages, can be found in the various doctrines of the intellect—the material or possible intellect, and the active intellect—all of which were derived from Aristotle's treatise *On the Soul*. We shall have to consider some of these theories, from the thirteenth century to the beginning of the fourteenth century, be-

tween Guillaume d'Auvergne and Duns Scotus. The first
reaction of a modern man when confronted with these
extremely complicated discussions is very simple; of what
importance, he asks, are these learned attempts to balance
entities? Let him look more closely. When men disagree on
the interpretation of particularly obscure Aristotelian texts,
some weighty problems will be found entangled in the intellectual controversies that ensue. The primary question
is one of relationships—of dependence and intimacy—between the thinking creature and his Creator; sometimes in
the passive, receptive character of human thought with
regard to the objects of sensory perception; or, on the contrary, of the spontaneity and transcendence of the soul in
its relationship to the sensory world; or again in the manner
in which our spiritual and intellectual being, having its
origin in the divine principle, is by that fact ready to return
to its source The intellect of the Middle Ages is a continuation of that of the Hellenistic period: to "understand"
was only its first function"; the second consisted in "com-
passing by itself" an incomprehensible God (A. J. Festu-
gière.) A conception of the life of the spirit, both for salvation and for knowledge, entered into these abstruse debates.

It is not surprising that we find this human interest in
abstract questions manifest when medieval men disputed
about man. But more often they reasoned about God. From
their point of view, it is true, both considerations were
closely united. The Middle Ages dealt with man as a
function of God, whose image he was thought to be:
"Trinitarian psychologies" correspond to theologies of the
Trinity; data from perception or from a rational analysis
of the mind become part of a mental structure recalling
that of the divine life. Sometimes remarkable for its precision and subtlety, this correspondence presupposes at least
an implicit answer to questions like these: To what degree
can the reflection of the human mind on itself enlighten it
about the nature of its transcendent beginning? Or, by
revealing Himself, does not a God who is said to have
created men in His image disclose something of the most

profound structure of their being, inaccessible to simple reflection?

The influence of ideas as theological as Trinitarian interpretations of the doctrine of man would be sufficient justification for not having omitted them from our study. The place this book gives to theology, it held in the mental regimen which we must describe in some detail. Our work ends on the threshold of the Reformation by touching on problems that divided Latin Christendom. These concluding pages will suffice, I think, to indicate how significantly an acquaintance with medieval theology contributes to an understanding of the subsequent destiny of religious thought, the attitude of modern man toward life, and certain inner tensions in Western societies.

As an element which integrates the past and present, it may be observed that the theological mode of thought still lives on and is revived among our contemporaries. It is sufficient to cite only the name of Karl Barth. This great theologian, moreover, has written an excellent book on medieval history: we owe much to his *Fides quaerens intellectum,* not only for an understanding of St. Anselm himself, but of all his successors who give to the intellectual history of the Middle Ages its decisive character. This work, moreover, leads to Barth's *Dogmatics,* where, in a Reformation theology absolutely committed not to degrade itself into philosophy, there appears a certain continuity with scholasticism, a discipline of elucidation in the presence of a body of teaching, an examination that refuses only "false prophets."

Confronted with these theological concepts, we must finally recall that, although religious feeling and the idea of God envisage a transcendent reality, they are nevertheless present in man. The value judgment of the philosopher and of the believer, from which the historian endeavors to make an abstraction, is of little importance here. Several remarks on this point will again suffice. On the other hand, as one scholar has written with reference to the doctrine of Port-Royal: "Whatever its origin may be, religious thought in itself is necessarily human thought, and therefore it should not be unimportant to men" (Jean Laporte); or, as has been said about the influence of mystics on modern philosophy: "It would be vain to presume that all that is capable of taking on a rational meaning must necessarily enter the world and the human mind by way of natural reason" (Victor Delbos).

What characterizes the notion of Christian philosophy is an influence of Christianity on speculations that wish to be rational. This poses a graver problem for the believer than for the unbeliever. It is the former who, in order not to make void faith by destroying the transcendence of its object, must reject the extreme judgment of Lessing's formula: "Without doubt religious truths were not rational when they were revealed, but they were revealed in order to become so."

Whether dogmas are conceived in terms of a final judgment as principles of life or obstacles to be surmounted, the values they postulate and the adherence accorded to them—since they are not alone in man—give rise to interior conflicts that appear not only in unbelief but even in the bosom of faith. We touch here on a theological dimension of the Middle Ages which renders that age less remote and which, in fact, brings it very close to us. Too often the Middle Ages have been imagined as being perfectly organic, completely harmonious, and somewhat rigid; at the bottom of its intellectual life we find agitation, discord, and division; that is to say, conflicts of the profane order with the sacred, a dialogue between the human and the divine. Whatever it is that suggests an oversimplified image of the Middle Ages as an organic age, it is not only in our own critical secular epoch that culture, in its collective reality, fails to offer ready-made solutions to the problems that affect its unity—the compatibility of the disciplines and the ideals that compose it, its harmony or conflict with religion. Synthesis doubtlessly imposed upon medieval men, as upon ourselves, a difficult personal task: an individual accomplishment was able to inspire novel attempts which the understanding of new data and the constant unfolding of history occasioned.

We have been led to the point of view we have just indicated by reflecting on "medieval humanism." In the first edition of this work, we noted that this expression—which is gaining general acceptance—is able to focus the center of our perspective on the intellectual character of the Middle Ages, if indeed it is possible at all to contain an entire epoch within the unity of a single perspective. The historian who has been trained in philosophy ought to fear excessive unification and systematization; unyielding diversity should be allowed to remain. He should not give the illusion of disposing of issues with a homogeneous certitude; it is for this reason that we have kept this resumé (insofar as it has been possible to do so) from assuming the appearance of an investigation—a mixture of assurance and scruple, both of which are subject to excesses. Here then, for critics prone to accusation, is the reserve and audacity behind our point of view.

Conscious of the partial character of this point of view, as well as of the inadequacy of the revisions made, after eighteen years, in the present edition, we have not felt it necessary to abandon it. The idea of humanism, applied to the Middle Ages, not only suggests tensions essential to the intellectual life, but also continuity with the ancient world, the classical dimension of the conception of man, and the human meaning of the natural philosophy brought by Aristotelianism. In the teaching of Duns Scotus, which has particularly attracted our attention, philosophical humanism goes beyond itself or rather is transformed into a theological humanism. More precisely, it becomes theocentric. That is, it represents a development in thought that exalts—*dignificare*—human nature by giving the greatest possible value to a finite being essentially turned toward the Infinite that alone can reveal Himself, and with this relationship bestows on the finite being its ultimate dignity and the destiny that makes it possible. Although capable of a God that he will receive through grace, medieval man remains a "nature in Nature" (M.-D. Chenu), in the center of an Aristotelian cosmos. Is the survival of Aristotle not due to his share in the definition of a humanity to be saved? Erasmus thought that Aristotle would have already perished by his time if he had not been "mingled with Christ." In an analogous passage, Etienne Gilson says that his metaphysics has survived as a result of the theological use to which Thomas and Scotus put it. He holds that in this way it was so transformed as to make it independent of an outmoded *Physics;* a work of human reason was allowed consequently to participate in the stability of "the light of faith," the place of its second birth. This paradoxical formula—the expression of an extreme point of view on "Christian philosophy"—provokes a question that can be asked in the realm of philosophical or theological anthropology (not having forgotten that for Duns Scotus the latter implies the possibility of metaphysics): What remains of the medieval notion of the condition of man and his nature, when it is juxtaposed to the discovery of the universe and of history in their modern dimensions? This problem concerns the whole of the West, whether Christian or not.

Even if we do not always agree with his interpretations, we must acknowledge here again what we owe to our master in medieval history, Etienne Gilson, to the precedent of his teaching, and to the immensity of his work, which is continually being revised. Our gratitude extends equally to all the scholars whose works we have used in writing this book, even though it has been possible to cite them only rarely; to the Fifth Section of the Ecole Pratique des Hautes Etudes, a privileged place for research; and to the Institut d'Etudes Médiévales of the University of Montreal, which has on several occasions given us the opportunity to revise this synthesis of medieval thought.

Chapter I

RENAISSANCES AND HUMANISM

The Middle Ages developed intellectually through the action of two renaissances—the Carolingian renaissance and the renaissance of the twelfth century. At the beginning of our study, moreover, a new aspect of the Middle Ages, namely medieval humanism, suggests itself. This unexpected juxtaposition of classical terms indicates several noteworthy facts which will clarify our understanding of both the medieval renaissance and medieval humanism.

The Carolingian renaissance spanned three reigns—those of Charlemagne, Louis the Pious, and Charles the Bald. Alcuin belonged to the first and John the Scot to the last. These two men should be remembered: Alcuin as a transmitter of culture, John the Scot for his proclivity to speculative philosophy.

The intellectual life of the Frankish empire was a continuation of that which had flourished in England in the preceding century. As Alcuin,[1] a monk of York who later moved to the Abbey of Saint-Martin in Tours, observed:

---

[1] Alcuin, born about 730, was called to the court of Charlemagne in 781 and died in 804.

"In the morning, while in the flower of my studies and my youth, I sowed in Britain; now my blood grows cold and it is almost evening, but I have not ceased to sow." It is interesting to note that Alcuin recognized the character of his work by the metaphor he selected to express his accomplishment. Asking for Charlemagne's aid, Alcuin writes that henceforth not only in York "but also in Touraine the trees of Paradise will grow and bring forth their fruit. Then the Auster, which blows over the gardens of the Loire, will come and spread its fragrance everywhere." A eulogy of the sovereign in another letter defines Alcuin's ideal: to build a new Athens in France, which will be superior to the ancient city since Christ will teach in it. As taught by Plato, the first enjoyed the brilliance of the seven liberal arts; however, the seven gifts of the Holy Spirit will raise the second above all earthly wisdom. With these two sevenfold entities we enter into the spirit of the Middle Ages. The disciplines that formed the first seven were grammar, dialectic, and rhetoric (which together made up the *trivium*); and arithmetic, geometry, astronomy, and music (which comprised the *quadrivium*). These seven liberal arts formed the culture to be transmitted. A chronicler, writing twenty-four years after the death of Alcuin, decided that his work had been successful; the "moderns," Gauls or Franks, he says, are equal to the ancients of Rome and Athens. Three centuries later, Chrétien de Troyes will express this same idea of the continuity of civilization:

> Ce nos ont nostre livre apris,
> Que Grece ot de chevalerie
> Le premier los et de clergie.
> Puis vint chevalerie à Rome
> Et de la clergie la some
> Qui or est an France venue.[2]

[2] [From our books we have learned that formerly Greece held the first place for chivalry and learning. Then chivalry and the highest learning came to Rome, from whence they have passed to France.]

By the end of the twelfth century, the city on the Seine will indeed seem to be the new Athens, and writers will speak of the way that culture has passed to Paris—*de translatione studii usque Parisium.* Various texts show that the Middle Ages preserved the idea of a cultural transmission from the ancient world. But let us put aside the word "culture" (if German sociologists will persist in considering culture as something unique and incommunicable) and think rather of the idea of civilization connected with the unity of human nature. Alcuin sees himself as having a quite natural affinity with the ancients. In his dialogue *On Virtues,* for example, he has them teaching Charlemagne. Since virtue, knowledge, and truth are valuable for their own sake, Christianity esteems and cultivates them. The dialogue continues with the student asking: "And the philosophers?"—"They knew that these things belonged to human nature and they cultivated them with great care."—"But then what difference is there between such philosophers and Christians?"—"Only faith and baptism" is the answer. Thus the value of ancient wisdom is recognized; the philosophers present man to the Christian simply as man; for medieval men, who distinguished themselves from the men of antiquity only according to the order of grace, the ancients had defined the nature of man. After the accomplishment of the transmission itself, there exists the possibility of communication. The first result of our inquiry, therefore, is this idea of a relationship, slightly different in hue but consistent, between the Middle Ages and antiquity.

Alcuin supplies us with a general idea of the Carolingian intellectual milieu from which John the Scot[3] has been too often isolated. John annotated Martianus Capella's *The Marriage of Mercury and Philology,* an abridgment of the seven liberal arts widely used in the medieval schools. He

[3] John the Scot (Johannes Scotus Erigena, often referred to simply as Erigena), born in Ireland in the first quarter of the ninth century, was master of the palace school before the middle of the century, and disappears from history about the year 870.

intervened as a dialectician in a quarrel about predestination; knew enough Greek to translate the works of the Pseudo-Dionysius and the commentaries of Maximus the Confessor (or John of Scythopolis) on them; and a treatise on man by Gregory of Nyssa. His translations, his commentaries, and his own original speculations in the *De divisione naturae,* permeated as they were with the influence of the Greek Fathers, constitute a glimpse of the East that will never cease to amaze and inspire the Latin Middle Ages.

In the eyes of medieval men, the author of the works of Pseudo-Dionysius (who is also referred to as Denis, Denis the Areopagite, or Pseudo-Denis, and whom modern scholarship has been unable to identify) was a convert of St. Paul and a confidant of the Apostle. This accounts for the exceptional authority which this Christian disciple of Proclus enjoyed, although it is probable that he wrote at the beginning of the sixth century. In the version of John the Scot and others, the complicated works of Pseudo-Dionysius present a picture of the celestial world and a conception of the spiritual life that deeply influenced, in a variety of ways, the mentality of the Middle Ages. The doctor of the *Celestial Hierarchy* and *Ecclesiastical Hierarchy* presents "a hierarchical world in which distinctions between its various levels are never obliterated," where even intelligences are assigned a place, according to the schema that late Neoplatonism, with Denis the Areopagite as its first intermediary, communicated to the Middle Ages. In a system of hierarchical knowledge in which light descends from above, intellects turn themselves toward the supreme principle with a view toward divinization. Consequently the Areopagite is also the doctor of mystical theology; a Bonaventure or a Gerson will think of him as a master. His Neoplatonic influence on Christian mystics poses serious problems, for the interpretation of this mysticism, with respect to the central role of Christ and the supreme position of the Trinity. On the one hand, the incarnation of the Word would seem to permit—without intermediary—a direct contact between man and divinity, "the presence of Christ in the intimacy of the Christian conscience" (R. Roques).[4] While on the other hand, at the end of the spiritual ascent, once the divine names are repudiated, the ultimate union can be seen either as "participation in the current of divine life" which is essentially trinitary (A. Stolz), or, by "the offensive return of Platonism," as fusion in "the primordial Unity" of Plotinus (Lossky), beyond the Trinity of Christian dogmatics.

For John the Scot as for Denis, the search for truth is confounded with the interpretation of Scripture. The Greek and Latin Fathers are the interpreters of the sacred texts, but their human authority is not the same as divine authority; proceeding from reason, the former is inferior to the latter. Too often scholars have spoken of rationalism here, when the only concern is to understand Revelation in circumstances where it is admitted that understanding presupposes faith and that there is nothing to seek beyond the meaning of the divine word. The theological significance of the Bible, that which refers to the divine, is determined dialectically. As the art of discussion—*disciplina bene disputandi*—dialectic deals with substances; it is concerned with the nature of all things which it separates in order to put them together again—*divisio naturalis omnium, substantiarum omnium collectio.* One finds the grammarian's taste for formal oppositions in the famous fourfold division: *natura—quae creat et non creatur—quae et creatur et creat—quae creatur et non creat—quae nec creat nec creatur.* The first and fourth instances, nature uncreated that creates and that which is neither created nor creates, represent the same God, the beginning and the end of everything else, but their distinction indicates that Creation manifests the transcendence of an invisible Absolute at rest beyond the Creator. In the third and second instances, with nature created but not creating and that which is both created and creating, we come to

[4] [For modern authors cited in this manner, see the Bibliography, beginning on page 215.]

beings and their archetypes; by qualifying them both as creatures, Erigena places the Ideas below God. Condemned in 1210 and in 1225, in the first ferment of the thirteenth century, the *De divisione* will be attacked again in 1241, when the University of Paris will prohibit the denial that men and angels see the divine essence in itself in eternity and the admission of eternal truths that are not God. These condemnations must not make one disregard either the influence of John the Scot, even though he was proscribed, or his quest for a satisfactory understanding of the word of God.

As a theologian, John looks only for God; in all things, he says, nothing can be seen except Him—*nil aliud in ea intelligas nisi Ipsum.* The attitude that we have observed in Erigena with regard to Scripture he maintains with respect to all forms of knowledge, both of the intellect and of the senses: whether visible or invisible, there is in each a "theophany" through which the divinity is more or less apparent. All things proceed from God in the same spirit as the words of the Bible; that is, in order to make Him known. Creation here means manifestation, revealing to the mind the God whom even the angels cannot see without such a revelation. The Ideas—such as Goodness, Essence, and Intelligence—are likewise creations, but they are one degree above those beings which participate in them. Of God it can even be said that he "creates himself," to express the idea that he manifests himself. At the same time that it makes the paradoxes of Erigena comprehensible, the concept of theophany, as a typically medieval state of mind, serves as an introduction to universal symbolism. Gilson has defined this point of view extremely well: "The natural world in which we live is of exactly the same order as that of Scripture, and the meaning of things is exactly the same as that of the Psalms or the Prophets," their function being to bring us back to God.

To this idea of a return in a cosmic sense, John the Scot gives the name of *deificatio:* beings which are transfigured and divinized serve no further purpose than to manifest God. After the end of this world, all nature, whether corporeal or spiritual, will appear to be *only* God; man will rise above his own proper nature, which will no longer be apparent, and God alone will remain. Erigena recalls the First Epistle to the Corinthians [15:28]: "that God may be all in all." In order to explain this deification, Maximus the Confessor furnished him with two metaphors: molten iron seems to be fire; illuminated air cannot be seen, but only the light that illuminates it. This is only a matter of appearances; we *know* that the iron and air remain. In this same fashion, only God will be seen; however, the integrity of the various natures will remain—*naturae integritate permanente.* Following Maximus, John the Scot makes this extremely important reservation. Later St. Bernard will make use of it again. These precautions, however, were in vain, for historians see in the *deificatio* a kind of pantheism. But why do they insist that creatures lose themselves in the same divinity in which they are saved? Let them listen to Erigena's explanation that inferior things are in effect naturally attracted and absorbed by superior things, not in order to cease to exist but rather, in the end, to possess greater being: saved, subsisting, and being made one—*Inferiora vero a superioribus naturaliter attrahuntur et absorbentur, non ut non sint, sed ut in eis plus salventur et subsistant et unum sint.* Let us conclude, then, that for all natures there will remain that which constitutes each one as an entity —*naturarum igitur manebit proprietas.* In spite of the scheme of return there is an irreversibility in the course of things; these natures at one time created and one day transfigured, are never destroyed. In the twelfth century, Hugh of Saint-Victor will be more perspicacious than the historians of the nineteenth century. This Augustinian moving toward the vision of God realized the degree to which John the Scot separates us from God by declaring that he is unknowable except through theophany; that is, a manifestation of divinity, distinct from divinity itself. In the *De divisione naturae,* no intellect, not even an

angelic intellect, apprehends the divinity without these
intermediaries; God who appears in all things remains *in
himself* absolutely inaccessible. It is impossible to imagine
a more radical distinction in the order of understanding.
By rejecting the thesis of Erigena, Hugh gives the common position of the Middle Ages, according to which the
ascent of the spirit terminates only with the actual vision
of the divine essence. The same God is *immediately* our
beginning and our end. Outside of Him there is nothing
to make us eternally happy just as there is nothing except
Him to create us—*ut non sit aliud extra ipsum, in quo
beatificemur, sicut aliud esse non potuit praeter ipsum, a
quo crearemur*. We return as we proceed, without intermediary; coming out from God, *exitus;* return to God,
reditus; the order in theology for Thomas Aquinas will
consist in following this tradition. According to a remark
of Bréhier, both the "Christian and the Neoplatonic view
of the universe have in common a sort of rhythm" of procession and return; but Christianity presents "a series of
events, each of which begins with a free initiative—Creation and Fall, redemption and future life in beatitude."
The *De divisione* introduces this sequence of events into
a dialectic that seems to demand the recovery of the
original Unity as the end. But how can the Incarnation,
an innovation concerning God himself, be fitted into it?
Such is the dimension of the problems that were posed
in the ninth century.

Hugh of Saint-Victor has carried us into the twelfth
century. The tenth and even the eleventh centuries are
dark and obscure ages, when learning was transmitted by
only a few schools. But at least an ideal was preserved;
and midway in this period, Pope Sylvester II, the celebrated Gerbert, gives a statement of it: "Since the ordering
of morality and self-expression are both inseparable from
philosophy, in my study I have always joined the art of
living well with the art of expressing myself well"—*Cum
ratio morum dicendique ratio a philosophia non separentur,*

cum studio bene vivendi semper conjunxi studium bene dicendi. Here again is medieval humanism. To use this expression is to refuse to accept the old definition of the Middle Ages as a period characterized by a scorn for the world, the famous *contemptus saeculi.* In such a proposal there is nothing new, since it is impossible to reduce the character of any age to a single quality. But before insisting on this humanistic aspect, let us deal first with its opposite, which is never absent and which sometimes predominates.

St. Peter Damian (*c.* 1050) is the very incarnation of the monk's scorn for the world. In his treatise on monastic perfection, the Law of Moses determines the treatment to which the Christian must submit philosophy and the corpus of profane learning before using them. Like the captive woman in Deuteronomy, "she shall shave her hair, and pare her nails; And she shall put off the raiment of her captivity from off her, and shall remain in thine house, and bewail her father and mother a full month: and after that thou shalt go in unto her, and be her husband, and she shall be thy wife." Peter Damian even fears the charms of grammar; the devil knows how to make use of this discipline. For had he not said: "You will be like gods"—*Eritis sicut dii.* It was from the tempter that our first parents learned to decline the noun "God" in the plural. The tract of Peter Damian against "the monks who stand on their heads to learn grammar" finds its rightful place in a long tradition of similar works. An abbot of the ninth century, Smaragdus, had confronted the authority of the grammarian Donatus with that of the Holy Spirit. In the first half of the thirteenth century, the Dominican Fishacre will again take up the fight against those who practice grammar under the pretext of studying theology, casting his aspersions in the form of a biblical simile: these people have devoted themselves for so long to worldly knowledge, in the guise of simple servants, that they offer themselves up to the embraces of their mistress only when, as old men, they can no longer beget anything;

and the woman whom they have ignored is none other than divine wisdom herself, who is "more beautiful than the sun."

Today it is difficult to realize why the grammarian incurred the wrath of these mystics for whom we ourselves can admit a certain enthusiasm. The history of philosophy preserves the metaphysical views of medieval authors, but it leaves aside those formal disputes that are so far removed from our own mentality and without interest for us. One ought not to forget, however, that the customary training of these men was both grammatical and logical. St. Anselm wrote a treatise on grammar concerned with the question: *An grammaticus sit substantia an qualitas?* Is the grammarian a quality or a substance? In the eyes of the great theologian, this sort of exercise imparted a knowledge of the art of discussion as well as of thinking. Before such practices came to be considered futile—a process that required several centuries—this technique not only interested men but even impassioned them. This can be better understood if we remember that in applying the grammarians' rules to Scripture, a man of the tenth century was dealing with the word of God in human language. A contemporary theologian, M.-D. Chenu, explains this well: "In its time, the grammatical method of reading the Bible provoked the same anathemas that the historical method provoked in the twentieth century."

If the invasion of grammar provoked such a conflict between the human and the divine, what can be expected of the dialectic method, similar in many respects, as we shall see, to grammatical speculation? The eleventh century witnessed the condemnation of two dialecticians: Bérenger de Tours, for his views on the Eucharist; and Roscellinus of Compiègne for his teaching on the Trinity. Medieval reason, once it had a new technique at its disposal, applied it directly to the realm of religious concepts —as we have already seen in the case of Erigena—the realm which was for the medieval mind the "immediately given." The arguments in favor of dialectic were the same as those which supported reason. In order to justify this discipline, Bérenger de Tours cites not only Augustine's eulogy of the dialectic method but adds: "Recourse is gladly made to dialectic in all matters, for to have recourse to dialectic is the same as having recourse to reason; therefore, he who does not utilize dialectic, having been made in the image of God according to reason, scorns his own dignity and cannot restore himself to the image of God from day to day." The anti-dialecticians drew their strength from an exclusively religious sentiment: a Christian, and especially a monk, ought to think of his salvation; the profane arts presented dangers to distract him, to turn him aside from this one task which alone was necessary. Thus dialectic, although weak and vain in our eyes, presented itself at that time with a humanistic value.

The logical-grammatical technique, one of the original creations of the twelfth century, constitutes a lasting trait of medieval man. The expropriation of the ancients appears where we least expect it, in the mystical school of Cîteaux, which was animated by a redoubtable *contemptus saeculi*. Indeed, to the astonishment of historians, "St. Bernard and his mule" were not in any sense strangers to the renaissance of their own century. Grammarians, however, did not indulge only in abstract theory; they also studied those authors who might serve them as models, Ovid in particular. The profundity of his influence was such that William of Saint-Thierry, a Benedictine who later became a Cistercian, thought of the *Art of Love* while writing his treatise *On the Nature and Dignity of Love*. But this mystical work was in fact written against Ovid and has been called an *Anti-Nasonem*. Profane schools had taught pagan love; in contrast to this, the cloister initiated monks into the school of charity—*schola caritatis*. But the memory of the classics lived on in this rude school in which the only master was Christ; a man lays aside his culture only with great difficulty. As an illustration of this, it is sufficient to observe the literary style of St. Bernard himself, with its use of classical expressions, puns, antithesis, and alliteration. Not only are classical themes encountered in Cistercian literature, but sometimes they are utilized for the expression of important ideas. A case in point is the famous "Know thyself," which was transmitted more by St. Ambrose and St. Gregory the Great than by St. Augustine. William of Saint-Thierry associated the Delphic maxim with a passage in the Song of Songs: *Nisi cognoveris te, o pulchra inter mulieres, egredere*—"If thou dost know not thyself, O most beautiful among women." (In the symbolic interpretation of the famous poem, Christ invites the soul to recognize its dignity, the image in itself of its Creator.) Cicero, too, serves for the interpretation of the Song, a fundamental text for these mystics. If Ovid's kind of love cannot enter a monastery, the Ciceronian *De amicitia* plays an important role. There one finds an exaltation of disinterested affection, based on similarity, that consists in the harmony of two wills; the union of the soul with God is of the same order, a *consensus*. Another Cistercian, Ælred of Rievaulx, relates that in his youth, which was given over to the delights of love, he found in Cicero a lofty expression of friendship. After he became a monk, living a new kind of life unknown to the pagans, he reworked the *De amicitia;* but his *De amicitia spirituali liber* remains faithful to the Ciceronian ideal: *amicitia est rerum humanarum et divinarum cum benevolentia et caritate consensio*—friendship consists in agreement on human and divine things in good will and charity.

It cannot be said that the "schools of charity" were directed by uncultivated monks. But what of the other schools? The cathedral school of Chartres was the most characteristic of the century. Let us try to revive something of its atmosphere. First of all, there is a sense of continuity with the ancient world. Bernard of Chartres says that we are dwarfs seated on the shoulders of giants; if we perceive more and see further, this is due neither to the sharpness of our own sight nor to the height of our bodies but rather to the stature of those who take us up and lift us to their gigantic height. Thierry, Bernard's younger brother, composed an encyclopedia of the seven arts. We read in his preface to this *Heptateuchon:* "The Greeks gave the name *Heptateuchon* to a manual of the seven liberal arts. Marcus Varro composed the first of these among the Latins, and after him came Pliny and Martianus Capella; they have drawn from the sources. As for ourselves, we have arranged, both with care and order in a single corpus, not our own works, but rather those of the principal doctors in arts; and we have united and, as it were, wed the *trivium* to the *quadrivium* in order that the noble tribe of philosophers may increase. The Greek and Latin poets hold, in effect, that Philosophy was solemnly betrothed to Mercury in the presence of the entire retinue of Hymen, with a concert given by Apollo and the Muses and the attendance of the seven arts, as though nothing could be done without them. And this is not without design. The philosopher needs two instruments, his mind and his means of expression; his mind is enlightened by the *quadrivium,* while his expression—elegant, reasoned, and ornamented—is furnished by the *trivium.* It is clear then that the *Heptateuchon* constitutes the proper and unique instrument for all philosophy. Philosophy is the love of wisdom; wisdom is the complete comprehension of the truth of things as they are, a comprehension that can only be obtained in the state of love. No man then is wise unless he is a philosopher." Such is the style of this introduction to the corpus of knowledge.

Teaching was evidently based on transmitted texts, and the medieval teacher was called a *lector.* For religious instruction, the reader "read" the Bible; in the profane order, let us cite Thierry's principal authors: Donatus and Priscian in grammar; Cicero in rhetoric; Aristotle, Porphyry and Boethius (whom we shall encounter again later in discussing Aristotelian logic in the twelfth century) in dialectic; Boethius again for arithmetic, music, and geometry. The section on geometry includes a fragment from

Adelard of Bath, a great traveler, who was one of the first translators to introduce into the West the science of the Greeks as transmitted by the Arabs.

Other elements in the culture of Chartres were two additional treatises of Boethius, the *De consolatione philosophiae* and his *De trinitate*. There was even something of Plato, a fragment of the *Timaeus,* as translated by Chalcidius together with his annotations on the same text. From these sources and from several others (Macrobius and Apuleius, for example), the scholars at Chartres derived a Platonic vision of the world. Thierry composed a treatise on "the work of the six days" in which the *Timaeus* is used to explain Genesis. Another work of the school, the *De universitate mundi,* written by Bernardus Silvestris and dedicated to Thierry, reveals this same double influence of Plato and Scripture. In this poetic cosmogony, where philosophical terminology does not interfere with a care for style in the manner of the classics, Providence prepares the events about which the poets will sing; it fixes the birth of Thales, Cicero, and Vergil, and predestines Christ; we are present at a dialogue between a *Nature,* which entreats a Trinity, and a *Nous,* which is the Word of God. Should we try to determine the doctrine of such a poem or leave it with its ambiguity, as expressive of a state of mind? A pupil of Bernard of Chartres, William of Conches, still thought of Genesis when he glossed the *Timaeus,* while another scholar, Gilbert de la Porrée, also a logician and theologian, apparently elaborated a metaphysics of forms.

In addition to the Platonism, the respect for the men of antiquity, and the encyclopedic character of the school which we have already discussed, the works of William of Conches reveal another characteristic of the thinking of the school of Chartres; without forcing the term too much, it can be said that there is certain "scientific" quality or tendency in his works. This refers not to William's atomism but rather to his basic attitude toward the *trivium* and the *quadrivium*. When they are taken together as verbal arts, grammar, dialectic, and rhetoric constitute eloquence; while arithmetic, music, geometry, and astronomy constitute philosophy. The latter deals with things as they are: *philosophia est eorum quae sunt.* . . . The authority of a quotation from Cicero, according to which eloquence becomes obscure if wisdom—that is, philosophy —is not joined to it, was used to denounce the vanity of false masters who do not progress beyond the first stage of knowledge. In short, it may be said that there is a tendency, in the school of Chartres during the twelfth century, to connect mathematical disciplines with Platonism. But the intellectuals of the time oriented themselves differently, not only turning away from belles-lettres, but directing their attention toward dialectic and the philosophy of Aristotle.

Chartres was supplanted by Paris. At the beginning of the century, Paris was already the city of dialectic: "Finally I arrived," Abelard tells us, "in Paris, where there already existed the tradition of cultivating this discipline to the highest degree." And Abelard himself, as a logician, was the glory of the Parisian schools.

Beginning with the different arts as the basic material for an encyclopedic culture, a problem of balance among the various disciplines presented itself. One approach to this question can be found in the *Didascalion* of Hugh, a master in the Parisian monastic school of Saint-Victor. Hugh does not forbid the study of any of the profane disciplines; "Learn all things," he counsels, "and then you will see that nothing is useless; for knowledge with reservations gives no joy." He goes on to explain the solidarity of the arts and how each must be studied in turn, for without this totality no one can be a philosopher. With less gravity and greater charm, this same care for balance can be found in John of Salisbury, who studied in both Paris and Chartres, and ultimately became bishop of the latter see. A perfect example of a cultivated man in a classical age, John asks of the New Academy that it achieve both the style and the wisdom of Cicero. An admirer of the *Topics,* he sees "the Philosopher" in Aristotle the logician, but he also perceives the inanity of dialectic, which "when left to itself, becomes bloodless and sterile."

This is the place to be precise about the state of Peripatetic logic in the twelfth century. At first not all of the *Organon* was available. The first twenty years of the century knew only the *Categories* and the *Peri Hermeneias* of Aristotle, and Porphyry's *Isagoge,* all translated and commented upon by Boethius. Later these three works will be referred to as the *logica vetus.* Between 1120 and 1160 the *logica nova* came into circulation: the *Prior* and *Posterior Analytics,* the *Topics,* and the *Sophistic Arguments.* These, too, were Latin versions from the Greek; they were the work of Boethius, who, in the twelfth century, appears most fully in his role of a transmitter. This transmission of Aristotle's works omits the treatise *On the Soul,* the works on natural philosophy, and the *Metaphysics,* which will arrive later via the Arabs along with the body of Islamic commentaries on Aristotle; the appearance of these works in Europe during the course of the thirteenth century will open a new era of medieval thought. But for the moment let us linger in the period that knew Aristotle only as a logician; without the eighth book of the *Topics,* says John of Salisbury, "disputation is not by art but by chance." What really mattered was to be able to discuss according to rules. But on what object should the virtuosity of the mind be exercised? Always the answer is the same: on the world of faith in which Christians live. Later we shall see Abelard pass from logic to theology. Of all the disciplines the Middle Ages received and appropriated for itself, dialectic became the essential technique. But its application to religious problems was not an empty game. A form of logic that has lost for us all of its freshness enchanted the men who discovered it; indeed it is the renaissance of the twelfth century that gives rise to scholasticism. After that it will scarcely be possible to speak of a literary humanism; thought will be expressed in an abstract style, impersonal formulas will hide interests which can remain living and even violent. Are there not in speculations of this kind occasions for conflicts between the human and the divine, conflicts of which we have already had a glimpse? When noting that ancient disciplines like logic and even ethics tend to be revived with an autonomous life, one can ask, utilizing the words of Alcuin to preserve something of the state of mind of the Middle Ages, what becomes of the brilliance of dialectic, the foremost of the liberal arts, in souls that are filled with the seven gifts of the Holy Spirit?

Chapter II

FOUR FOUNDERS:
St. Anselm, Abelard, St. Bernard, Richard of Saint-Victor

To discuss in some detail several of the founders of scholasticism, we must make a selection, realizing that any choice is arbitrary in some degree. St. Anselm indubitably dominates his age, the second half of the eleventh century. But in the twelfth century, alongside of Abelard, there is a place for Gilbert de la Porrée, another master of matters logical and divine—*in logicis et divinis.* Among the mystics, adversaries of the dialecticians, the doctrinal work of William of Saint-Thierry without doubt rivals the better-known writings of St. Bernard. In the school of Saint-Victor, which reconciled mysticism and dialectic, Richard, whose speculations on the Trinity we will note because of their originality and influence, was preceded by Hugh.[1] Let us devote our attention to four founders

[1] A few dates: Gilbert de la Porrée was bishop of Poitiers from 1142 to 1154; William of Saint-Thierry, born about 1085, died

with the realization that it would be better not to be limited in this way.

St. Anselm[2] has taken his place in the history of philosophy as the inventor of that proof for the existence of God that Kant called ontological. From century to century, philosophers have disagreed as to the value of this mode of argumentation; historians are still divided over its original meaning. It is with some hesitation then that we discuss this famous text from the *Proslogion*. The numerous commentaries provoked by these few pages, however, furnish us with a good illustration of our own difficulty in acquiring a medieval point of view for grasping problems. Let us try to forget all later speculation, even that of the thirteenth century; let us particularly avoid classifying Anselm's argument according to any preconceived idea of different kinds of speculation—for example, the distinction between *philosophy*, seen as the autonomous operation of reason, and *theology*, where the certitude of the conclusions is based on the principles of faith. St. Anselm did not categorize his work according to our concepts. He did, in fact, relate his *De veritate*, a work that seems philosophical to us, to the study of Holy Scripture— *studium sacrae scripturae*. This treatise begins with the words: *Quoniam Deum veritatem esse credimus . . .* ("Since we *believe* that God is Truth . . ."). With at least as much reference to the fundamental notion of faith, the *Proslogion* belongs to the same class; its preface informs us of the rather unexpected purpose it was meant to serve: "the study of Holy Scripture."

The *Proslogion* is actually a continuation of the *Monologion*, which Anselm defines as: *exemplum meditandi de ratione fidei*—an example of meditation on the rationality

---

about 1148; Hugh of Saint-Victor, born in 1096, taught at the Abbey of Saint-Victor in Paris from 1125 until his death in 1141. With Gilbert, one might compare Alain de Lille, who was born about 1128 and died in 1202.

[2] Anselm was born in Aosta (Italy) in 1033. Entering the Norman Abbey of Bec in 1060, he became prior in 1063 and abbot in 1078; from 1093 until his death in 1109 he was archbishop of Canterbury.

of faith. This soliloquy introduces us to a mind which searches while reasoning, while disputing with itself. A form of dialectic, in short, whose ideal the monks of the Abbey of Bec had imposed on their prior Anselm. Compelled by the necessity of rationality not to leave any objection without reply, he sought to persuade them of absolutely nothing—*penitus nihil*—by the authority of Scripture. The *Monologion* and the *Proslogion* seek to establish by necessary reasons—*rationes necessariae*—and not by the testimony of Scripture, all that a Christian believes about Nature and the divine persons. These writings leave aside the Incarnation but include the Trinity; they are not concerned with a philosopher's God. We must understand the paradox of a study of matters of faith that seeks to discover reason and necessity for them. These *rationes necessariae*, famous in medieval history, have several characteristics: they do not in any sense present themselves as a force without peer, but admit of an authority with even greater power (*major auctoritas*), namely the Gospel and the Church; they are offered to an intellect in the course of a dialectical search which assumes at least the *form* of a dialogue; they are not, however, mere probabilites for the use of this or that questioner, but rather aspire to the universality of the true. Eadmer, Anselm's biographer, calls them "*invincibles.*" Let us pass over the question of their necessity, in order to understand this concrete indication of an atmosphere of discussion.

The *Monologion* is generally remembered for the proofs of the existence of God given in the first chapters. The concepts on which these arguments are based undoubtedly seem typical of the mentality of the Middle Ages: the participation of the objects of human experience in the good and even in being, a participation that is unequal in degree and finite in number. But by considering only these proofs, and by including in the essence of the Creator a doctrine of divine attributes, seen as Ideas, a "natural theology" is extracted from Anselm's tract, a treatise "on the one God" as distinguished from a treatise "on the triune God," the subject of "revealed theology." Would it not seem that to apply these distinctions to the *Monologion* is to shatter its dialectical structure and to disregard its purpose?

The twelfth century saw the *Monologion* as a *De trinitate*. The speculative chapters on God are for the most part devoted to the Word, to the Father, and to the Love or the Spirit that proceeds from one to the other. Whether they deal with the Trinity or the unique essence, the necessary reasons follow one after another, and are all equally compelling; the continuity is not broken by the divisions that are traditional in theology today. Between the proofs for the existence of God and the discussion of his attributes, the idea of the "word" is introduced by the notion of Creation: Is the word interior to the supreme mind, and what is its relationship to the essence of God? Once the identity is established between the attributes and this simple essence—so transcendent that in the sense that it *is,* everything else *is not*—the mental word by which the Creator speaks of His eventual creatures is seen as the Word that is consubstantial with the supreme Principle. *Ecce quaerenti mihi de verbo quo creator dicit omnia, quae fecit, obtulit se Verbum, quo seipsum dicit, qui omnia fecit*—an examination of the word by which the Creator says all that He has done, leads to the discovery of the Word by which He calls himself the One who has done everything. This phrase embodies the experience of a kind of dialectical ascent of which we know no other example; Anselm's attempt consists in making clear the necessity of finding the Word that is God—*locutio consubstantialis*—by beginning with a word—*locutio rerum* —that merely expresses the things to be done. At the point of departure, the image of the artisan, rectified but not eliminated by the concept of *ex nihilo* creation, suggests that before being made things were *said* in God, by an interior word that constitutes the model: *forma, exemplum.* This "exemplarism" does not develop into a theory of

Ideas, immediately identified with the divine essence, but
—through a progressive purification of the initial an-
thropomorphism—it becomes a doctrine of the Word, at
first distinguished from the creating Principle, finally separating from it to be recognized as consubstantial.

It is not possible to explain here how this discovery of
a Word, a Son in the presence of a Father, develops itself into that of the Holy Spirit. Let us only remember
that as a result of Anselm's dialectic the supreme unity is
forced to admit of a plurality as inexplicable as it is inevitable—*tam ineffabilis quam inevitabilis probatur esse
pluralitas.* The proof does not remove the mystery, it remains impenetrable—*impenetrabile secretum*—the more
so because we do not reason directly about the divinity;
whether it is a question of the word or of love, we grasp
something of the divine life only through a consideration
of its image in our soul. By reflecting on this characteristic
of the soul, St. Anselm not only finds the basis for the
possibility of reasoning about God, but also the obligation
of turning toward Him as the end of love, hope, and faith;
this obligation is inscribed in the very nature of the
image, related in an essential way to its source. The proof
of the *Monologion* is concerned not only with the content
of belief, but also with the kind of adherence its object
exacts: *credere in*—with a faith implying love. There
must be an undivided belief in a certain unity and trinity:
the unity of essence—(*propter unam essentiam*), a trinity
that seemingly is more obscure—(*propter tres nescio
quid*). "Three I know not what": this lack of proper
terminology to indicate the Trinitarian realities characterizes the situation in which dialectic recognizes and
justifies the language of the Church, certainly necessary
considering the divine object, as well as the poverty of
human language and thought. The God, then, that men
must adore is one and three; this is the conclusion of the
Monologion.

But the author was dissatisfied with the sequence of
reasons he had developed; to establish the existence of a

"sovereign good that has no need of any other," he sought a proof worthy of its object and in its image, "a single argument which, to be proven, needs nothing but itself alone": to the *summum bonum nullo alio indigens* corresponds *unum argumentum quod nullo alio ad se probandum quam se solo indigeter.* The preface of the *Proslogion* reveals a dialectician who wants a self-sufficient argument which, as a proof, equals its object in perfection. Anselm despaired of finding it, and wished to renounce his attempt, but ultimately he knew the joy of discovery. At first Anselm thought of giving the result of this dramatic search a title which would perhaps cover his entire work, faith in search of understanding—*fides quaerens intellectum.* But instead he decided on *Proslogion,* "allocution." We hear the voice of one who seeks to understand what he believes, lifting his spirit up toward contemplation. For this believer, the dialectic of divine things, together with the comprehension of them, comes to occupy a place between his belief in God and the face-to-face vision of God to which, in the hereafter, he aspires. Thought is operative in a realm between faith and vision—*inter fidem et speciem.* An understanding of this fundamental situation makes it possible to comprehend not only Anselm's speculation but later scholasticism as well. To discourse according to rational necessity finds its place between believing and seeing, but both belief and vision are products of grace —that is, divine gifts.

A prayer precedes the argument and forms the first chapter of the *Proslogion.* It should not, however, be considered merely as a vague piece of pious rhetoric, a banal call to contemplation; rather one may find in it the human environment that gave birth to the proof. It is a dialogue between the creature and his Creator: *quaero vultum tuum* . . . "I seek Thy countenance," the desire to see the face of divinity in a being—in ourselves—created precisely for this vision. Although we were created for this, we have never yet experienced it. The possibility of this vision was lost, for the entire race, by the first man; original sin

explains the absence of God. The monk sees in his need
for the divine vision the universal lamentation of the sons
of Adam, a sort of worldly sorrow. The problem for
Anselm—and for his followers—was to recover something
of man's understanding before the Fall, partially to re-
establish man in the state from which he had fallen. But
to remake what has been destroyed, to accomplish a sort
of re-creation, is a superhuman task, the work of grace:
hence the prayer of the speculator. It must not be forgotten that for Anselm man cannot seek if God does not
teach him, nor find if God does not manifest himself.
Doce me quaerere te et ostende te quaerenti—"Teach
me to seek Thee, reveal Thyself to him that seeks Thee":
such is Anselm's request. But a mind about to reason is
not something passive. The office of grace is to give form
to the divine image that has been effaced in man; in this
resemblance, a constituent part of our nature, there exists
the power to think of God. Anselm's prayer requests a
renovation of one of our faculties.

The problem of the *fides quaerens intellectum* is not
immediately cast in intellectual terms; the ascent must be
made by love. We must not equate the human mind with
the divine being. Quite free from any such pretensions,
Anselm's intention is this: the believer desires to view
darkly in the present the transcendent object that he hopes
to see in another life, to anticipate the vision of the future
by means of reason. Let us dwell on this point: Anselm's
very formal argument begins with sentiment. This historical fact makes one skeptical of the validity of the
common assumption that mysticism and scholasticism—religious sentiment and logical rigor—are opposed to each
another. To understand the Middle Ages, the historian
must beware of such categorization. Dialectic born of
love aims only for an *aliquatenus intelligere,* not for a
penetrare—some measure of understanding, but not pene-
tration. The *Monologion* set forth the idea that to formulate
rationes necessariae, it was not necessary to understand
why things were so, to penetrate the *quomodo ita sit,* to

grasp the object by its internal possibility. The individual manner of being is not fathomed; it is dealt with in terms of some analogy. Anselm's necessity deals with a hidden essence: *Nihil de hac natura potest percipi per suam proprietatem* ("By means of what is proper to it, nothing concerning this nature can be perceived"); this is a fundamental and frequently revived theme. The Trinitarian God of speculation remains a mystery of faith. Let us remove from our minds the ideal of a Cartesian meditation: deduction through a sequence of evidences, in which the possibility of a thing would be seen in each step, and in which to prove His existence, the very idea of God positively indicates that He is the cause of Himself. This dialectic does not revel in such light; it utilizes an indirect but compelling procedure.

Faith lies at the point of departure for the intellectual quest: "I do not seek to understand in order to believe, but I believe that I may understand. For *I believe* I cannot understand unless I believe." Has it not been said: "Unless you believe you will not understand"? St. Anselm merely sought to follow this precept which, after his perusal of St. Augustine, he found in Isaiah: *nisi credideritis, non intelligetis.* Lanfranc, his master, had been the adversary of Bérenger; he himself will staunchly oppose Roscellinus. In his opposition to these dialecticians—rash to the point of heresy—he seeks to re-establish dialectic in its rightful place, in the order of things beginning with faith. With reference to an object of belief, it is never possible to posit that it might not be; rather, never ceasing to affirm and love it, a search is made for a reason why it is true. If he arrives at such understanding, the Christian will enjoy it; if not, he will venerate what he cannot grasp. Thus the same method that in principle does not prohibit speculation on any religious matter, recognizes as a result of experience that certain matters evade it; understanding is a gift that God measures out for us according to His inclination. In this way Anselm's faith, undisturbed by any difficulty or impossibility in understanding, is left intact. It would be wrong to imagine an unbeliever asking reason to make him believe, or even troubled believers who, by strengthening their certitude, relieve themselves of doubt. The prior of Bec wrote for his Benedictines, who hardly resembled such individuals. This then is another aspect of the medieval mind: a very firm faith in quest of precise rationalization. A final spirit of prayer, at the threshold of the argument, determines the subject for speculation: God exists and is just as we believe him to be.

The idea of God about which he proceeds to reason is given to St. Anselm by faith: *Et quidem credimus te esse aliquid quo nihil majus cogitari possit.* "We believe that Thou art something *than which nothing greater can be conceived*"; neither a scriptural nor a traditional divine name can be recognized in this expression. Rather an Augustinian theme already revived at the end of the *Monologion* is again encountered here: the necessity of adoring God as a being so supreme that nothing greater is conceivable. This maxim of Christian sentiment becomes a rule for thought. An intelligence that realizes the sense of the word *Deus* according to Anselm's formula will not discover the real dimension of divinity, the "grandeur" in the sense of "loftiness," *altitudo* as the first chapter expressed it. The third chapter will offer an explanation: If a mind were able to conceive something better, the creature would raise himself above the Creator by whom he would be judged. That is to say that the idea of which we treat carries its object beyond itself: the fourteenth chapter will show that in the *aliquid quo majus cogitari nequit*, "that than which nothing greater can be conceived," there is a *quiddam majus quam cogitari possit* ("something greater about which it is not possible to think"). Occupying as a creature a position below the Creator, what can we place under His name? An essence, it has often been said. In the sense of every definable object, the "content" of thought? We are confronted with something that thought cannot contain. In the sense that only God is Being? The *Proslogion* considers God in this way only after his existence has been established. The proof begins with a signification: If we speak of the "idea" of God, we must be precise and say that here the idea of God possesses only the negative aspect and logical function of an essence. But it is not in any sense something fictive or arbitrary, incapable of tying us down; rather it is given by faith as a rule for thought. Anselm's *De veritate* defines truth as rectitude: the language conforms to the thought, the thought to the thing. In following this conception, it is possible to compare the idea to a regulatory power, to a potentiality of mental action. All of Anselm's work is clarified when he explains to his critic Gaunilon the difference between a *majus omnibus quae sunt* and a *quo majus cogitari non possit;* he says that "something greater than all that which is" would need something further to establish its existence. But is a determination of this kind not relative with respect to essence, as the *Monologion* had pointed out? It does not seem so, for when one wants to think of God absolutely, according to His dignity, one moves in the direction of a logical dynamism so radical that the object of the proof is also the means of the proof—*de se per seipsum probat.* What is proven about Him is proven by means of Himself. The originality of the *Proslogion* consists in having converted the Augustinian concept of absolute divine grandeur into a dialectical principle such as this.

Unaltered in the course of a deduction which moves directly from one evidence to another, dialectic preserves its fundamental characteristic of a disputation. Scripture provides Anselm with his adversary: "The fool has said in his heart, there is no God." This is not a case of any problem whatsoever disputed among philosophers; the dialectician is confronted with the unbeliever who denies the existence of the God of faith. It is difficult to deal with the question of the place of the infidel both in Anselm's works and with respect to medieval speculation in general, which sought to "prove" religious truths. Briefly it may be said that the unbeliever is not directly addressed by St. Anselm, but he is nevertheless a person not to be overlooked. Those works that necessarily begin with a datum of faith are written for believers: the prior speaks to his Benedictines. But if they demand reasons to resolve all their objections, his quest will assume the form of a discussion, and the antagonist will enter upon the scene. Let us not think of man purely as man, outside of all revelation, which is either accepted or rejected. The matter for debate is the object of faith itself. The adversaries are the believer, who accepts it, and the unbeliever, who rejects it. The first is bound to the second: fulfilling not only the *Nisi credideritis non intelligetis,* the believer satisfies another requirement derived from a sacred text; the First Epistle of Peter expresses the wish that the faithful be always ready to give anyone a reason for the hope that they cherish: *parati semper ad satisfactionem omni poscenti se rationem de ea, quae in nobis est, spe.* In the fifteenth century, "the last of the scholastics," Gabriel Biel, will once again define the office of the theologian in these terms. Some twenty years after he wrote the *Proslogion,* St. Anselm cites this passage in the *Cur Deus homo.* This treatise indicates that the study of faith should devote some place to the objections of the infidels and gives a noble expression of the unity of all men, however divided they may be with respect to revelation: "The unbelievers seek a reason for their unbelief; we seek to justify our belief; what we both seek is 'however one and the same." *Unum idemque:* one object, the datum believed or to be believed; the same question: its rationality. In effect, a resolution has been made not to have recourse to authority, but rather to move in the realm of the necessary, or as one might as well say, the universal. Without having "abandoned," as Karl Barth has said, "the shelter of the Church for one instant" in order to seek some common ground, the author of the *Proslogion,* while addressing his monks, speaks against the unbeliever.

Unbelief does enter into the *fides quaerens intellectum:*

having defined the God of faith, the inquirer finds His existence placed in question by the denial of "the fool." He proceeds to answer this question; the negation will become a part of his dialectic. The adversary must enter the game. When Anselm expresses his formula, it is heard and understood; the unbeliever thinks that *that* does not exist at all, but *that* does exist at least in his thought. When this *esse in solo intellectu* has once been admitted, the mechanism of the proof unfolds by itself: "That than which nothing greater can be conceived cannot exist only in the intellect. For if it were only in the intellect, one could also conceive that it had existence in reality which would be greater. Therefore, if the being than which nothing greater can be conceived existed only in the intellect, then this same entity than which nothing greater can be conceived is something about which something greater can be conceived, and this is clearly impossible." Modern men, frequently looking underneath for some hidden foundation of the argument, have little taste for this technique. Nevertheless, that is the text; it is found, moreover, in other passages of the *Proslogion,* as well as in later works that follow Anselm's method. Between the first chapter and the statement of the proof there is an amazing change: pure mechanism follows upon animated thought. Technicality of this sort is another characteristic of medieval thought.

To understand this intellectual situation, let us grasp the problem as it developed. In the inner realm of thought, there are different possibilities: the believer considers the existence of God; the unbeliever denies His existence. To close the one will be to open the other. The reduction of the adversary to a contradiction is always the tour de force of dialectic. In this case, there is an aspect of originality in Anselm's procedure: beginning with a minimum (God *in solo intellectu*), something more is conceived (God *in re*), and it becomes necessary to admit this maximum. St. Anselm and "the fool" have accepted the same notion of divinity: the one, with faith, the other by refusing to accept it. This idea constitutes a rule: it is impossible to think of anything beyond God; our thoughts have to remain on this side. This is not a question of mere sentiment, however strong it may be, but of a strict rule by which the formalism of the argument is expressed. The mind is moved by constraint. The argument, moreover, has the appearance of a refutation: the existence that at first seemed to be denied is finally asserted beyond all doubt; the objection, which constituted the negation, has received an answer.

After this apparently indubitable proof has been given, the truth of the existence of the divine being is made more specific and singular in the following chapter, which proceeds from a *sic vere est* to a *solus igitur verissime omnium:* at the beginning, God truly is; at the end, of all beings, He *is* in a supremely true way. Here we are confronted by a unique quality: "This being than which nothing greater can be conceived truly exists in such a manner that it is impossible to think that He is not." The mode of existence determines the mode of thought. Historians have seen in this attitude the objectivism of the *De veritate,* by which all true thought presupposes the reality of its object. It ought to be observed, however, that the text does not have its origin in the impossibility of doubting the necessity of being; it continues by dealing in the same way with the meaning of divine "grandeur." The existence of God is not a prerequisite for giving a reason for what we inevitably believe: this is not a pre-Cartesian metaphysics of the cause of ideas. Anselm's method is always dialectical, ascending now toward a kind of contemplation. *Et hoc es tu, Domine Deus noster.* "And that is what Thou art, Lord our God." In this Being which constrains the mind not to deny Him, St. Anselm recognizes the God of the Church and of his faith: "Thou art then, Lord my God, so truly that no one can think that Thou art not"—*Sic ergo vere es, Domine Deus meus, ut nec cogitari possit non esse.* In the order of thought, a real presence appears. By means of the proof, the believer attains understanding.

Being in the highest degree is possessed only by that which cannot be conceived not to be. What creates a problem is not its existence but rather the negation of this existence. "Why has the fool said in his heart, 'There is no God,' when it is so clear for a rational intellect that Thou art more fully than all others? Why, unless it is because he is stupid and foolish?" This is the question posed by the believer, before his God, with respect to the scriptural fool. The answer is given by the question itself. The following chapter raises another that receives a lengthy reply: the question is not *why,* but *how;* it is no longer *cur dixit,* but *quomodo dixit.* To interpret this, we must not imagine that we are dealing with pure philosophy; what should be noted is the profound impression the fact of unbelief makes on the believer. It suffices to recall the perspective of the original prayer: humanity that destroyed itself requires divinity to restore it. After the integrity of the mind, received at the time of Creation, has been lost, this can be accomplished only by a will requiring no other reason than itself. Elsewhere St. Anselm suggests that he willed it because he willed it—*voluit quia voluit;* this formula reappears during the Middle Ages in all cases where a will appears as an ultimate principle. On the one hand, God does not re-establish all men in their original perfection, He does not "reform" all men; some of them He abandons. In the course of the *Proslogion,* this choice appears to be supremely just, although it remains incomprehensible: His reason why cannot be fathomed—*nulla ratione comprehendi potest, cur. . . .* The man who lacks grace, the man to whom grace is lacking—we cannot separate the two. It is sufficient for us that the denier of God is conceived in a similar context: there is no *why* that can explain his negation.

But for the dialectician who has shown this to be unthinkable, one question still remains: "*How* can the fool say in his heart what he cannot think?" Considering thought in terms of interior speech, the answer establishes a relationship of meaning that links words to things: the *voces-res* relationship, remarkable in the dialectic of this period, which we shall encounter again in Abelard. Concerning a single thing, one can either think the word that signifies it, or understand what the thing itself is, *idipsum quod res est;* the mind acts in a different way according to whether it stops with words or whether it realizes their significance and thus turns toward things. Let us recall that St. Anselm has *stated* a definition for God: "that than which nothing greater can be conceived," and that his adversary had to admit that something understood or conceived was in the intellect. We are in a scheme in which a thought is linked to language, where faith has determined the meaning of the word "God." One who follows the rule could not conceive that the object is not; but he can however express the word "in his heart," either without any meaning at all or else with an extraneous meaning, *aut sine ulla aut cum extranea significatione.* In such a way the believer represents the mental state of "the fool," and the *how* of the negation. While holding to the truth, he has explained the possibility of error: what more could be asked?

In the name of the "unbeliever," Gaunilon, a monk of Marmoustier, takes up the controversy; to his *Liber pro insipiente,* Anselm replies with a defense for his proof in the *Liber apologeticus.* Historians have seen in this discussion, among other things, the beginning of the classical debate on the idea of God in the ontological argument. Let us only remember that since "the fool" refuses to receive the notion of divinity from faith, Gaunilon asks in his name if it is possible to think of God according to what he is, *secundum rem.* This can only be done verbably, *secundum vocem:* hearing the word puts the mind in motion and forces it to formulate a meaning; truth would then be discovered only by chance. When one speaks of another being, a man for example, the process is totally different: either reference is made to a certain man whom one has seen, or an image of another is formed on the basis of the former. In the case of God, the thing itself is not known and there is no longer any possibility for conjecture about it on the basis of a resemblance to something else. This reality, which is not given to us, can no longer conform to our genera and species: no representation, let us say, can in this case realize the sense of the word. In the first lines of his answer, Anselm labels his adversary *catholicus pro insipiente* ("a believer who speaks for the unbeliever"). The Christian is asked to admit to himself that he thinks of God as that than which nothing greater can be conceived: "I appeal to your faith and to your conscience as my strongest argument." The perception of faith is sufficient to constitute the idea that forms the basis for the proof. On the other hand, Scripture teaches the believer that the invisible perfections of God are made visible to the intellect by the works he has performed—*invisibilia Dei per ea quae facta sunt intellecta conspiciuntur*. This passage from St. Paul will compel medieval philosophers to seek a road toward God that begins with the sensible; here it permits St. Anselm to remind Gaunilon the Catholic that it would be impossible to grant that the *insipiens* cannot conceive of divinity through conjecture. Anselm undertakes to demonstrate that it is possible to formulate the idea of God that he has received through faith by beginning with the data of common experience; once this idea has been constituted, the argument follows its course. Since it begins with faith, the argument of the *Proslogion* is theological in character; by virtue of a different point of departure, it becomes a philosophical proof in the *Liber apologeticus*. These texts seem to suggest a way to solve a dilemma—a proof can be either theological *or* philosophical. After Gaunilon's objection has been set aside, the argument of the *Proslogion* remains valid just as it is: It is sufficient to have denied the God of faith to fall under the rule that determines how He should be conceived; "the fool" is completely refuted.

A refutation places us between two adversaries. One of them finds a reason for what he believes, but what about the other? We, who live today, would like to know what effect this dialectic was thought to have on him. I do not know what St. Anselm would have told us. He does not seem to have been primarily concerned with the efficacy of his argument in this sense. Between faith and understanding, the unbeliever appears merely as an interlude in the quest of the believer, in order to provoke a dialectical discussion and keep him faithful to his ideal, while beyond recourse to the Gospel or the Church. This then is a characteristic which will reappear again; in the mind of the medieval Christian, the idea of the unbeliever carries with it the need for a certain rigor which serves to test the purity of arguments. Anselm's arguments tend toward a logical structure, independent of any authority, universally valid; they are by no means dependent on reasons accessible only to faith.

The same objective datum takes on a different sense in another spiritual situation, however. Perhaps this remark makes it possible to deduce, without too great a risk, the position of the unbeliever with respect to the proof. In the mind of the believer, he occupies a place between faith and understanding. How can understanding be found when faith is lacking? For the maxim is imperative: *nisi credideritis non intelligetis.* Not only has St. Anselm obeyed these words, but he has sought to understand this datum that is also a matter of faith: "He who has not believed cannot understand; for he who has not believed has not experienced, and he who has not experienced cannot understand, for just as the experience of a thing surpasses *the fact of hearing it spoken of,* so *the knowledge of one who experiences* outweighs the understanding of one who only hears." If the understanding of the believer is seen as a *scientia experientis,* the unbeliever, confronted with the same proof, finds himself reduced to the *auditus rei;* his understanding of this matter for which a reason has been given comes only by hearsay. Without leaving a faith he cannot communicate, the Christian answers questions from the outside. Having attained understanding, he gives thanks: *quod prius credidi te donante, jam sic intelligo te illuminante, ut si te esse nolim credere, non possim non intelligere.* "What I at first believed by the faith Thou hast given me, I now understand because Thou hast enlightened me, to the point that if I did not want to believe that Thou art, I could not comprehend it"; the divine object manifests itself under the appearance of something necessary. Through dialectic, the mind obtains a first satisfaction of its desire, together with the means to lift itself higher, to the point of having a presentiment of "the joy of the Lord," the immensity of which St. Bonaventure will note. It is not without cause that A. Stolz has spoken of mystical theology in connection with the argument of the *Proslogion.*

The influence of St. Anselm will scarcely be apparent to the thirteenth century; that of Peter Abelard is more immediate and more glittering. When his name falls into oblivion, his spirit will have become a part of the intellectual regimen, for this great professor of logic was the founder of a school in theology.[3] A knight of dialectic, he lived in battle. He triumphed over his masters, taking their pupils from them and carrying them off for himself. When he applied logic to religious matters, he was twice condemned. His art was also his undoing: *odiosum me mundo reddidit logica.* Logic, which made him hateful to the world, did not exhaust the interests of a man almost as rich and variegated as his century. A poet, he has left

[3] Peter Abelard, born in 1079 in Le Pallet (near Nantes), taught by turns at Melun, Corbeil, on the Ile de la Cité and Mont Sainte-Geneviève in Paris, at Laon, and then again at Paris, where his adventure with Héloïse took place. In 1121 came the first condemnation at Soissons and in 1141 the second condemnation at Sens. He died in 1142. Anselm of Laon died in 1117, William of Champeaux in 1121.

us some religious verse; in honor of his beloved Héloïse, he also wrote some love poetry. A humanist, he savored the beauty of the ancient classics; from the maxim "Know thyself" he derived the title for his treatise on ethics— *Scito te ipsum*. He extolled the teaching and life of the philosophers, who did not seem to him to be too far removed from Christianity; he wished Plato had known the Trinity, and during part of his career he sought to explain how the mystery could be understood by pagans. But all these profane sentiments did not obstruct his faith; his confession of it to Héloïse is still famous: *Nolo sic esse philosophus, ut recalcitrem Paulo; nolo sic esse Aristoteles, ut secludar a Christo.* Let us not make any comparisons between a modern rationalist and this man who declares: "I do not wish to be a philosopher to the point of resisting Paul; I do not wish to be an Aristotelian to the point of being separated from Christ." The pace of his life can be found in his work; this professor, whether in favor or embattled, was a busy man. The works he published he never ceased to revise; several times he re-worked his logic, several times his theology. If today his theology benefits from a "sort of rehabilitation" (J. de Ghellinck), it is because of these revisions. More important is the atmosphere in which his thought developed: we are in the midst of scholasticism.

The treatise on logic, *Ingredientibus* (the title comes from the first word of the manuscript), deals with the famous problem of universals. Let us forget the "conceptualism" that nineteenth-century historians bestowed on our dialectician and preserve the terminology of the period. In contemporary texts the thesis of Abelard is called *sententia nominum;* his disciples are referred to as *nominales.* We must determine the meaning of this "doctrine of names," this "nominalism," unrelated perhaps to later nominalism. In his introduction to Aristotle's *Categories,* translated and commented upon by Boethius, Porphyry poses, but does not answer, certain questions about the genera and species used by Aristotelians to classify beings—for example, do they really exist or are they only in our minds? Both constitute universals which medieval Latin Aristotelianism defines as *quod de pluribus natum est aptum praedicari*—"those things whose nature permits them to be predicated of several subjects." As logicians, we are dealing with propositions; the universal is seen as a term. But Aristotle, Porphyry, and Boethius, the authoritative authors in logic, speak of genera and species not only as words, *voces*, but also things, *res*. To translate *vox* is not without difficulties: let us preserve for our "word" the concrete, physical character of something spoken. *Est autem vox, Boethio teste, aeris per linguam percussio . . .* —"there is a word, according to Boethius, when the tongue strikes the air. . . ." To this let us add the idea of signification: *significare autem vel monstrare vocum est*. Abelard adds: *significari vero rerum*. In effect, the property of words is to signify or to point out; but the property of things is to be signified. The problem of universals is defined in this context; being established in language, among the signs that denote realities, one asks oneself if the definition of the term "universal" can be applied to things themselves. There are several methods of proceeding with this application. Abelard examines and rejects all of them; here his criticism overtakes his master William of Champeaux, a scholar of the cathedral school of Notre-Dame in Paris.

By asserting the impossibility of saying, logically, that things are universals, their nature is defined. An epitaph praises Abelard for having shown not only *quid voces significarent*, but also *quid res essent*—"what words signify" and "what things are." There is in his nominalism a simple, but clear, ontology. His adversaries—we will call them the "realists"—imagine that in the interior of each being there is a core of some universal substance or essence—*man*, for example, in Socrates; singularity would result from superimposed forms. But even if all these accidents were to be removed, the thing would still remain an individual entity—*omnibus etiam accidentibus remotis in se una personaliter permanet.* Individuality is fundamental and permeates the entire being. Forced to abandon his first position, the realist vainly tries to explain that the same Socrates can be seen from two points of view: he can be visualized either as what he is in *himself* as distinct from all others, or in terms of how he *does not differ* from certain others; in the latter case, *man* becomes a universal. But for Abelard the nominalist, nothing can, at a given moment, be different from itself, for whatever it has in itself, it has in utterly the same way—*nulla enim res eodem tempore a se diversa est, quia quidquid in se habet, habet et eodem modo penitus.* Because of this radical singularity of things, there is no way that what is in one can be in another—*nec ullo modo quod in una est, est in alia.* If, between two things that resemble each other, it is impossible to find in one what is found in the other, their resemblance cannot be realized in any manner apart, nor does it in any way consist in some third reality: Socrates and Plato correspond in the fact of being man; but the fact of being man is not a man, nor is it anything else —*conveniunt in esse hominem. Esse autem hominem non est homo, nec res aliqua.* Let us agree that Abelard does not reduce genera and species to pure fictions; he believes in the classification of beings based on the real. Certain historians have attempted to make him a precursor of the "moderate realism" that has commonly been attributed to St. Thomas Aquinas. But as we shall see, his position with respect to realism coincides with that of William of Ockham; the great nominalist of the fourteenth century will not express the individuality of every *thing* with greater vigor or clarity.

The universality that things themselves reject we can only attribute to words—*restat ut hujusmodi universalitatem solis vocibus adscribamus.* Grammarians distinguish between proper nouns and common nouns; dialecticians divide terms into universals and singulars. Here again, the terminology is of great importance, and unless we explain it with considerable precision, we run the risk of not understanding Abelard and others who followed him. "Noun" can be used to translate *nomen;* "term" to render *simplex sermo,* the part of speech called *oratio.* In *In-gredientibus,* universals are indifferently called *voces, nomina, sermones.* There does not seem to be any distinction between Abelard's "nominalism" and the *sententia vocum* (doctrine of words) taught, according to contemporary witnesses, by Roscellinus, who was also one of Abelard's teachers. John of Salisbury, however, says the two theses are opposed to one another, just as *sermo* is to *vox.* And the opposition of the two is confirmed by another of Abelard's treatises on logic, the *Nostrorum petitioni sociorum* (again the first words of the text). Here too, *nomen* appears as a synonym for *sermo;* their common sense is clarified by examining the definition of the universal: *quod est natum praedicari de pluribus, id est a nativitate sua hoc contrahit, praedicari scilicet*—"whose nature consists in being predicated of several things; that is to say, that which by the act of its birth contracts the property of being predicated." The expressions *natum* and *nativitas* suggest to us the possibility of grasping the nature of universals in the act from which they proceed; language was invented through the initiative of men. *Quid enim aliud est nativitas sermonum sive nominum quam hominum institutio?* What else is it in fact that gives birth to terms and names, if it is not their institution by men? Here again, the distinction between *nomen* or *sermo* and *vox* is apparent. The latter now seems to be of the same order as *res: vocis vero sive rei nativitas quid aliud est quam naturae creatio, cum proprium esse rei sive vocis sola operatione naturae consistat*—the act which gives birth to the word or the thing can only be the creation of nature, since the very existence of the thing or of the word consists solely in the operation of nature. Let us here recall the physical character, the physiological genesis of words in being pronounced. From this point of view, the word (*vox*) is itself only a thing, and as incapable of universality as anything else. Abelard says that neither words nor things are in any sense universals—*voces sive res nullatenus universales esse.* In his discussion of *nomen* or *sermo,* he specifies the one way in which our verbal expressions do constitute universals: it is only because they have received a meaning from us. Having determined *what things are,* he returns to *what words signify.* A brief but decisive ontology has revealed the impossibility of finding universals outside of language; this detour ends among *things,* with an orientation toward *terms;* universals are not derived from a science of the real, but from logic—*sermocinalis scientia.* In pursuing Abelard, the reader discovers the viewpoint of this science of terms, of discourse—a fundamental position for medieval men.

In order to understand theological works, so important for their influence, this frame of mind acquired in dialectic must not be forgotten. At the time Abelard's *Theologia* appeared, even the use of the word seems to have been new. At Laon in the beginning of the century, *divinitas,* a term Hugh will revive later at Saint-Victor, was used in the same sense that a theological school in twentieth-century English usage is still called a "divinity school." Similarly in the eleventh, twelfth, and thirteenth centuries, when the common religious study consisted in "reading" scriptural texts, they were called *pagina sacra,* and men spoke of teaching *doctrina sacra* (this same expression may be found at the very beginning of St. Thomas's *Summa theologica*). Let us briefly sketch the different stages in the development of this kind of study. At first, the sacred text was explained by the insertion of interlinear and marginal glosses; this was the procedure followed in the school of Anselm of Laon, where the elaboration of the classic medieval gloss was completed, and the same method will be encountered again in the sixteenth century in Luther's famous commentary on the Epistle to the Romans. But the Fathers and more recent authors were also read; as the method developed, some were content to make extracts in the course of their reading; others organized this material according to the arrangement of Scripture in order that it might be more easily used. Taken out of context, sometimes with little regard for the authors' original meaning, these thoughts and remarks constituted *sententiae*. These "sentences" were not only collections of notes on sacred texts; they also formed dossiers relative to various doctrinal debates. In the margins of Scripture, from the beginning of the Middle Ages, questions that required answers were asked. Eventually the essential tie to the text became rather tenuous and the discussion itself underwent a considerable development. We have already seen St. Anselm present his *De veritate* as an example of *studium sacrae scripturae;* elsewhere he speaks of *sacrae paginae quaestiones*—questions, we might say, posed by Holy Scripture. Scholasticism can be seen as a literature of questions. Beginning with a "yes" or a "no," dialectic comes into full play; the dialectician finds a problem for himself when *quaestio* is defined as *problema dialecticum*. To realize that in the final stage of this development the questions did not remain separate entities like Anselm's treatises, but tended to form an ensemble, to compose a system of the world and of life, these collections of "sentences" must be examined. Some of them, instead of following Scripture, attempted to achieve a more or less systematic order. This is what happened at the beginning of the twelfth century in the school of Anselm of Laon and William of Champeaux, and somewhat later in that of Hugh of Saint-Victor. Landgraf places the theological school of Abelard between these two; and alongside them, that of Gilbert de la Porrée. This tradition leads ultimately to Peter Lombard's *Libri sententiarum,* on which all theologians of the later Middle Ages, including even Luther, wrote commentaries. It is in this milieu, in this tradition, that Abelard's theology finds its proper place as a *sacrae eruditionis summa*—a *summa* of sacred learning. Let us hail this word which the thirteenth century will make famous.

Faith, along with divine authority, is the point of departure; one has no merit with God except if one believes in God, not in proofs devised by human reason, Scripture does not constitute the only source; the Fathers too are included, in their proper place. Question by question, the famous *Sic et non* arranges the *dicta sanctorum,* the opinions of the Fathers, authorities who affirm opposed to others who deny; the work of the sententiaries sets up the contradictions that the dialectician must resolve. The atmosphere of the school is in the process of formation. Canonists had already had to reconcile conflicting texts, each of which was valid; Gratian will complete the *concordia discordantium canonum.* The theologian works with similar data, attentive—he remains a dialectician— to the sense of the words. The majority of conflicts between authorities will resolve themselves, Abelard thinks, if it can be established that the same words take on different meanings in different authors. Characteristic of a frame of mind, the *Sic et non* was written after the condemnation of the *Tractatus de unitate et trinitate divina.* Abelard's students "demanded human and philosophical reasons, they had greater need for understandable explanations than for affirmations. They said that it is useless to speak if one does not convey the meaning of one's remarks, that it is impossible to believe what one has not first understood, that it is ridiculous to teach to others what neither the teacher himself nor those whom he teaches can understand." This account of the master puts us in the contemporary setting. We ought to remain there; when he speaks to us about "comprehension" or "understanding," he is not concerned with the reality of a mystery, but with the sense of the words that express it. Is it not the dialecticians' task to assemble terms and endow them with meaning? The *Tractatus* of Abelard criticizes Roscellinus, whose doctrines are not very clear to us; St. Anselm accused him of having posited that there were three Gods; it seems rather that he only asked if it was possible *to speak* of three Gods. Abelard appears to proceed on the same level; he seeks, it has been said, to prove that the affirmation: "God is three persons" does not logically entail saying: "God is three." His reasoning attempts to give a meaning to terms that allows certain liaisons. From what source does he draw these arguments? From comparisons and "similitudes" that are not in any sense equivalent to the thing itself. Seen as a whole, the ambition of his theology is modest enough: *non veritatem, sed aliquid verisimile.* Its object is not to attain truth itself, but merely probability concerning God. The comparisons relative to the Trinity were ill-fated, they brought forth the reprobation of the Church. Nevertheless Aristotelian logic—utilized only in part by Abelard—will become a part of *doctrina sacra.* It must be recognized that in the twelfth century these procedures seemed like completely profane innovations. A renaissance ardor accompanied the revival of the technical skills of dialectic.

As much as Peter Abelard, the glory of Paris, seems to be one of the founders of scholasticism, a master in the art of thinking, in the same degree this role would seem to be unsuitable for his adversary Bernard of Clairvaux.[4] Nevertheless the mysticism of this enemy of dialectic lacks neither unity nor rigor; Gilson has demonstrated the presence of a "system" in his work, an awareness of the relationship between problems and solutions. Let us not hold to an overly simplified idea of "mystical experience." Actually the data are received with an ever-ready interpretation, and the practice is dependent on principles; faith, which precedes the personal "intuition," is not in any sense a vague sentiment, but it has a definite content, the material for a doctrine. There is no need for the inventions of reason; it is enough to draw upon the treasury of Scripture and the Fathers—including not only Augustine, but Origen, Gregory of Nyssa, and Maximus as well, both the ascetic example and the theology of the Christian East: what William of Saint-Thierry called the *orientale*

[4] St. Bernard was born in 1091 and entered the Abbey of Cîteaux in 1112; subsequently he became abbot of Clairvaux, where he died in 1153.

lumen. St. Bernard merely advances what he has found in a tradition which, since for him it contains the truth, cannot but answer his questions in a coherent fashion.

In order to understand these questions and answers, let us recall the position of mankind that seemed fundamental to us in St. Anselm: *inter fidem et speciem.* We must insist on this division between the worldly and the otherworldly; the two are separated by a divinely established barrier, which in Bernard's judgment Abelard and the dialecticians disregard. The mysticism into which we enter finds its abode within faith and remains there; it is characterized by the humility of a mind constantly submitted to a hidden object. We must disabuse ourselves of any idea of intellectual intuition.

The Christian stands before his God as a creature in the presence of his Creator. The metaphysicians of the Middle Ages, for whom the notion of being constitutes a very lofty state, like to refer to the biblical passage in which God defines Himself in terms of being; from this a doctrine which Gilson has called the "metaphysics of Exodus" is derived. Present in St. Bernard, this notion of Being, embodied in Revelation, points out a serious difficulty for the problem of mystical union: "The same One who said: 'I am who am,' *is,* in the true sense of the term, since Being is what He is. What kind of participation or reunion can there be then between one who is not and One who is? How can things so different be joined together?" If we remain faithful to texts of this kind, we will not think that the medieval mystic went to great lengths to dissolve and lose himself in God; the creature and the Creator appear so different to him, in the order of being, that at first he does not know how they will be united. They must be united, however, for does the Psalmist not say: "It is good for me to adhere to my God"? Bernard attempts to suggest how this is possible: "As a being we cannot be directly united with God; perhaps this union can be effected through some intermediary." Since identity of essence is excluded, there can be union only through a middle term, that is to say, love.

Let us return to the situation of a man who recognizes that he is a creature. St. Bernard takes up the maxim "Know thyself," but St. Paul comes to supply the deficiencies in Socrates. In this "Christian Socraticism," we discover both what we are and what a divine gift is: the Epistle to the Romans teaches that it is possible to reach God through his works; why not lift ourselves up to the Creator by beginning with ourselves, since we are made in His image? This idea seems so natural that the failure of the pagans to have recognized the divinity is inexcusable. Created and knowing that he is created, man finds within himself a natural law: "He must love with all his being the One to whom he knows he owes everything." The realization of a debt so complete and radical demands a measureless love in return; consequently the distinction between creature and Creator is not only the cause of the distance that separates us from God, but also of the force that brings us back to Him. Above all other things, this love for God constitutes the true state of man, the integrity of his nature; if, in fact, this sentiment is lacking in him, such a deficiency, however profound it may seem, does not pertain to his essence but is an accident which needs to be removed. Hence the Fall and the Redemption.

The first man—Adam—resembled his Creator as an image and a likeness, both of which, for St. Bernard, are of the order of freedom. He distinguishes three different aspects of freedom: *libertas a necessitate, libertas a peccato, libertas a miseria;* the image consists in being free from necessity; being free from sin and misery—that is to say, from suffering—constitutes the likeness. The purpose of these distinctions is to define the present state of mankind relative to the condition of Adam before the Fall. Let us briefly explain each term of the analysis in order to understand where it begins and where it ends. First of all, we find the power to consent and to refuse consent: "Freedom from necessity belongs equally and indiscriminately to God and to every rational creature in general, to the good as well as to the bad. It is lost neither by sin nor by misery." Free will constitutes something indivisible: our human dignity resides in it; it is the divine *image* in us which nothing can destroy. The other properties admit of degrees and can be lost. These are the power to choose the good, to be free from sin, and the power to do this as something enjoyable, to be free from misery. The first man was free from both evil and the suffering experienced by not avoiding it. We, on the other hand, are incapable of not sinning, of not feeling the misery of this incapacity. In a remarkable fashion, inner experience is expressed here in theological concepts relative to the disposition of mankind before the Fall. The "freedom from sin" and the "freedom from misery," which together constitute a freedom of perfection, comprise the *likeness* in which Adam was created. We who have lost it, live in the "realm of dissimilarity." *Regio dissimilitudinis:* this expression, Platonic in origin, fits the circumstances of man the sinner. Remaining the image of God by his free will, but becoming dissimilar by evil and suffering, "how could the soul refrain from crying out: Lord, what is similar to Thee? Seized with despair by so great a misfortune [the dissimilarity], the soul is drawn to hope because of this great good [the image]. This is why the more it is displeased with itself, because of the misfortune in which it finds itself, the more ardently it strains toward the good which it also sees in itself, longing to become what it was made to be." Like the problem of understanding in the thought of the prior of Bec, the problem of love for the abbot of Clairvaux is concerned with the restoration of a fallen nature.

This restoration of man is the task of the monastery; in contrast to the schools where Plato and Aristotle are taught, the cloister returns to "the school of the primitive Church," where Christ is the teacher. In it, St. Benedict,

His minister, has organized the apprenticeship in charity, which passes through the twelve degrees recognized in the virtue of humility. Here again, there is an examination of conscience, of the knowledge of oneself. To understand this, let us try to realize the tension, in the "disfigured soul," between the image that remains and the likeness that has been destroyed: "While still confounded by your ugliness do not forget your beauty." Humility consists in this confusion, but it includes, let us note, the concept of a natural dignity. The novice learns to recognize his misery. But when he knows that, he knows the next stage as well —have not all the sons of Adam been degraded by the same Fall? The novice then takes up the road that leads from humility to compassion, the route on which his divine Master has preceded him: the Word in His divine nature, explains Bernard, has knowledge of man's lot, but before the Incarnation "He did not know it by experience"; what Christ as God knew from all eternity, He came "to learn through the flesh in time." Such is the paradox of the love that is manifested in the Passion. When confronted with this situation, the mystic soul says, with the Spouse of the Song of Songs, that it is "wounded by charity." The intensity of the love that wrought Creation is revived and augmented by the Incarnation.

He who is compassionate possesses charity. But what is charity? A quality of the soul, the gift of God, who is himself Charity: "It is equally true to say of Charity that it is God and that it is the gift of God; this is why Charity gives charity: the substantial [God] gives the accidental [the quality of soul]." A divine gift, love is seen as the sought-for intermediary between Being and ourselves. In this way, the Creator gives the creature the means to resemble him, and this resemblance is the basis for knowledge, the mystical knowledge of God. To be convinced of this, it is sufficient to reaffirm the words of St. John: "He who does not love does not know God, for God is love." Maximus the Confessor described this assimilation to the divine through love in the same phrase that John the Scot utilized. With John and Maximus, the mystic of the twelfth century has a framework in which to place *excessus*, ecstasy. If in this context he speaks of "knowing" or even of "seeing," these word ought not to deceive us. In contrast to the philosophers who conceive of a soul which, as a whole, has acquired knowledge, for St. Bernard a soul acquires nothing but love, in the fullest degree, in the possession of the object toward which it strives with all its being. In this life, pure feeling takes the place of the clear vision reserved for the hereafter; as a mystic, the Christian remains in the obscurity of faith. But completely immersed in divine love, the mystic finds himself freed from sin and "misery"; for the duration of his ecstasy, there is a brief enjoyment of the freedom of perfection, of the *likeness* refound. These indications suffice to show that a series of concepts taken from tradition come to encompass the experiences that Bernard and his disciples seek in their cloister.

To lend authority to the "necessary reasons" for the truths of faith, texts of the thirteenth and fourteenth centuries cite, along with Anselm, Richard of Saint-Victor.[5] Setting to one side his purely mystical works, including the *Benjamin major* which will inspire the *Itinerarium* of St. Bonaventure, let us concentrate on his *De trinitate*. It is impossible to overemphasize the fact that the God of the Middle Ages was conceived as a Trinity. The *Monologion*, as we know, passes without apparent effort or break in continuity from divine existence and essence to the plurality of persons; when speculating on the Trinity, Anselm follows the way indicated by Augustine: something of the Trinity must be found in the soul since it is a divine image; with respect to knowledge the analogue of the Word is sought, with reference to love some parallel with the Spirit. In Augustine's *De trinitate*, the Middle Ages found the revealed configuration of God linked with

[5] Richard, the student and successor of Hugh in the school of Saint-Victor, died in 1173.

the analysis of our soul. From this a number of "Trinitarian psychologies" were derived; Richard, however, does not follow this tradition. In the present state of our knowledge, he seems to move in a new direction. His dialectic, on the one hand, is applied to divine things (the eternity, the primary or derived character, and the incommunicability of the mode of being) with an abstract style that foreshadows Duns Scotus. On the other hand, he converts a spiritual theme—the traditional excellence of charity—into a proof of the Trinity.

Richard's *De trinitate* is reminiscent of the spirit of the *Proslogion.* "The just man," the Apostle has said, "lives by faith," from which hope and charity proceed. What will the fruit of charity be? Let us listen to Christ, in the Gospel of John: "He that loveth me shall be loved of my Father, and I will love him, and will manifest myself to him." This places us in a perspective that is directed toward the vision and likeness of God. Let us press on along the way: as much as God permits and as far as we are able, we must constantly strain to understand the object of our faith by reason. This is a complex frame of mind: for the true believer, faith constitutes an absolute certitude. Belief, however, is but a small part of the price of understanding; yet only souls firm in faith can attain understanding. The biblical text *Nisi credideritis non intelligetis* is always referred to. These men apply themselves to a task which, even if not completed, will have its value. Richard knows the articles of Trinitarian faith; he reads them, surrounded by authorities. But where are the proofs? He does not remember having read how they might be formulated. To establish the plurality of persons demands that much greater application and ardor since the Fathers give few principles in this matter for argumentation. "Seeing to what my quest aspires, let him laugh and scoff who will: it would be right to do so. For, to tell the truth, if I have the audacity to attempt it, it is rather more the result of being impelled by a burning soul than the consequence of being elevated by knowledge. And if it is not given to me to arrive at my destination? If I fail in my purpose? I will, however, have one joy: devoting my energy without stint to the quest for the countenance of my Lord, in having run, labored, and suffered fatigue." Note the emotional warmth, the haste to proceed; this is characteristic of Richard of Saint-Victor's style.

In a celebrated passage, the *De trinitate* lays the foundation for its proofs: God is necessary in himself; it is, by necessity, impossible that we should lack arguments to explain all that is—not only probable ones, but necessary ones—even if they evade our efforts to discover them. Having stated this much, Richard plunges into a dialectic as confident as that of Anselm. If the biblical "fool" was necessary to deny the God of the *Proslogion,* the mind itself is defective in the opponent of Richard's Trinitarian faith; this *mentis inops* is a *phreneticus*—an Augustinian term—a fool whom the believer attempts to convince with his arguments. It would be difficult to express the ideal of an irresistible proof in a better way. There is even a desire to indicate the progressive order of evidence by use of the comparative and superlative: *evidens, evidentius, evidentissimum.* Let us not think however that the *De trinitate* begins with the central light of an essence, whose properties would then be evident; having determined on the one hand the unity of substance, and on the other the plurality of persons, Richard encounters the difficulty of reconciling the two—a mystery remains for veneration.

Without describing the complex operation of this "contemplative dialectic" (Guimet), we can indicate a few of Its most important characteristics. In order that a dialectic so vital to its inventor does not appear empty, we must at once realize that for Richard the excellence of charity is, as it were, a natural datum derived from our conscience, enlightened by the Gospels and the Fathers. Let us say, with him, that there is nothing better, nor more delightful, nor more magnificent; in this way we express the significance of the triple point of view of goodness, felicity, and glory—the three things that God possesses in their fullness. There are three ways, in short, to envision charity, and consequently, altruism (Gregory the Great). If, as opposed to a private, individualistic love of self, its essence is to turn toward others, several, or at least two, persons must be admitted to the divine love. But although altruistic and "ecstatic," it remains ordered: *caritas ordinata* (Origen). The same demand of self-extension in love that commands us to love our neighbor as ourselves leads us to the idea that the love which is God must go out to some *other* being, not less divine.

Being given the plurality of persons, this constitutes their equality. But it is not enough for charity to be divided in two: mutual love must be shared by a third. Such is, in rapid review and accelerated to an extreme, the course of Richard's logic of divine sentiment. In twentieth-century terminology, it is a "social theory" of the Trinity: from the first moment of eternity, there is one person, admitting of absolutely nothing preceding himself; for that person, another, his equal, is necessary, whom he loves and who loves him; from this is derived the necessity of a third, also equal, so that their common love is not restrained in any way. From the Father, who is not preceded by anything in any way, is born an equal in dignity, the Son—*condignus*. From the Father and the Son proceeds one whom they both love at the same time, the Spirit—*condilectus*. Like a flood—*divinitatis unda*—divinity is a flux of love—*affluentia amoris*—emanating from the Father, received by and emanating again from the Son—*tam effluens quam infusa*—received finally by the Spirit.

Man finds his place in his relationship to these Three that are One in the same love, divided according to their titles in the possessing of it. The Father loves the two other persons, to whom He gives everything; this is a *gratuitous* love. The Son turns himself toward the Father, his source, with a love that is *due*, but on the other hand, the love of the Son for the Spirit, of whom He is the source, is *gratuitous*. The Spirit then, as the last person, only receives: He *owes,* as it were, all this love. Let us compare these nuances of divine love with our love for God: the charity of man, the sentiment of the creature for his Creator, is one that is *due,* like the love of the Spirit in the divinity. This Trinitarian theory enables us to understand a text from the Epistle to the Romans, an essential passage for medieval theology: "The love of God is shed abroad in our hearts by the Holy Ghost which is given unto us." Why does the Apostle speak of the third person, the Spirit, and not of the others? Because the sentiment of a creature, so radically a debtor, can only imitate a love that is *due.* And Richard tells us again that love is similar to a spiritual fire; the Spirit works on our heart, as fire on iron, which he transforms into His likeness. Once again we encounter a classic metaphor, even though the mystical relationship between the soul and God is dealt with in Trinitarian terms.

Chapter III

THE INTELLECTUAL ENVIRONMENT
OF THE THIRTEENTH CENTURY

Abelard has told us of his impatience to come to Paris,
the city of dialectic. John of Salisbury has enumerated all
the charms of that city: the abundance of victuals, the joy
of the people, the respect paid to the clergy, the varied
occupations of philosophical minds; he ends in mystical
terms: "In truth the Lord is in this place, and I did not
know it." Whatever may be the significance of Bologna,
the city of Roman and canon law, or the special role of
Oxford in the intellectual movement, the University of
Paris will keep the first place. In the capital of Philip
Augustus during the early years of the thirteenth century,
with the help of Innocent III, the corporation of masters
and students, *universitas magistrorum et scholarium,* came
to constitute a privileged body. The medieval University,
like the priesthood and the Empire, was considered an
organ of Christendom. We who live in national cultures
are struck by the international recruitment of both students
and masters; of the most celebrated of the latter, none,

from Alexander of Hales to Duns Scotus, was a native of
the French realm. One of the characteristics, then, of the
thirteenth century is this catholicity of the Parisian center
of studies—*studium parisiense*—the goal, as we have seen,
of the *translatio studii.*

The culture to be transmitted was developed in the
schools of the twelfth century; the great scholastics of the
thirteenth century are first and foremost Schoolmen, "con-
ditioned by professional techniques": they must be seen,
together with their works, in the framework of the University. The latter consisted of four faculties: this word,
originally applied to each discipline taught, designated both
teachers and students. Let us leave law and medicine aside
and devote our attention to the arts and theology.

The handling of logic and grammar in the faculty of
arts must be indicated because of the importance of these
disciplines for the formation of minds. The doctors of the
thirteenth century proceeded by means of questions; they
participated in disputes—some ordinary, on a subject determined in advance; others extraordinary, where anyone
present could propose questions on any subject. From the
first category come the *quaestiones disputatae;* from the
other, the *quaestiones quodlibetales* which we may read
today. In such a system, dialectic was mistress. We have
already noted the improvement resulting from the addition
of the *logica nova,* especially the *Topics,* to the *logica
vetus;* the particular influence of the *Analytics* in the
thirteenth century and later must also be considered. On
the one hand, it became necessary to juxtapose traditional
Christian teaching and the Aristotelian ideal of knowledge;
the classical question *Utrum theologia sit scientia?* was
cause for reflection on the nature of both theology and
science; on the other hand, a strict conception of demonstration carried with it a formidable principle of criticism
for the proofs that had formerly been admitted. For the
interpretation of Aristotelian logic, which in the twelfth
century had constituted "the old logic" and "the new
logic," the thirteenth century added "the logic of the

moderns." This *logica modernorum* was a systematic treatment of the properties of terms, as found in the *summulae
logicales* of Peter of Spain (who died in 1277 as Pope
John XXI). We will consider a section of this work—the
theory of the *suppositio*—apropos of William of Ockham.
Other parts were commented on during the thirteenth,
fourteenth, and fifteenth centuries by a variety of authors
with diverse metaphysical points of view.

As the logicians' technique developed, becoming more
complex, the grammarians moved more and more into the
abstract: they disassociated themselves from authors and
from concrete matters—the literary quality of language, for
example—in an attempt to give their discipline the appearance of a form of logic. The thirteenth century is
indeed, as Gilson has said, an age of "exile for belles-
lettres." This "speculative grammar" that envisioned a
universal structure beyond linguistic particularities, which
were considered accidentals, dealt with ways of signifying
—*de modis significandi*. Scarcely studied as yet, this logico-
grammatical material formed the substructure for great
speculative edifices, which, if they were better understood,
would doubtlessly explain more than one aspect of medieval
thought. As St. Thomas himself says, theology takes into
consideration not only things but also the meaning of
words, for to obtain salvation a vocal confession by names
must be added to a faith relative to the truth of things. It
is a part, I believe, of the structure of medieval thought to
deal with ways of speaking as well as with modes of being,
to pose questions *in voce* as well as *in re*. One might add
that these medieval verbal analyses are still of interest, as
the early work of Martin Heidegger on a fourteenth-century
doctrine of signification indicates.

Besides this development of disciplines of expression—
sermocinales artes—the attention devoted to new subjects
in the thirteenth century revived both the arts and theology.
Before dealing with the renovation of philosophical culture,
it is fitting to emphasize with M.-D. Chenu that the return
to Christian sources in the thirteenth century was another

factor in this cultural regeneration: the "evangelism" that manifested itself not only in heterodox sects, but also in the two Mendicant Orders in which the principal doctors flourished; the scriptural curiosity that sustained biblical teaching, "the scholastic exegesis," which is a rather neglected accomplishment of those same theologians (Thomas Aquinas, for example) whom we tend to remember only for their philosophical writing; the return to patristic sources, with a deepening of Augustine's influence, as well as of the "Eastern" inspiration of the masters condemned in 1241. Contemporaneous with the Aristotelian revival that has attracted so much attention, there was also a "revival of a faith nourished on sacred texts." In both instances, the activity of the University went beyond the work of the previous century. With the four books of Peter Lombard, the Master of the *Sentences*,[1] we return to a development we left with Abelard's *Sic et non*. The *Sentences* quickly became a standard textbook: at first it was glossed, later it was commented upon; in the universities of the thirteenth, fourteenth, and fifteenth centuries this exercise led to the academic degree of "Bachelor Sententiary." Luther himself annotated the *Sentences*. Although the explanation or exposition of the text itself was of little importance, the *Commentary on the Sentences* became the typical work of the medieval theologian. Questions, which were detached from it, were freely developed for their own sake and came to be arranged, in the tradition of the schools, according to the divisions or "distinctions" of each of the four books. Speculation moved then in the framework established by Peter Lombard according to the Christian perspective of the world and of salvation: God as the Trinity and creative activity, the divine work from angels to men, sin and Redemption, virtues and sacraments, beatitude— so many truths given by faith, which it would be im-

[1] Peter [the] Lombard, born near Novara, studied and then taught at Paris. He became the bishop of that city in 1159 and died *c.* 1160. The *Sentences* were written about 1150-52.

possible for reason to rediscover, as if she herself had invented them, since most of them are expressions of free acts. This simple enumeration is enough to remind us that the theologian's task consisted in reasoning about a "sacred history," and not about an order of essences.

At the very moment when the teaching of the *Sentences* was established, profane studies underwent a revival. With the exception of the Platonism of the *Timaeus,* the Middle Ages up to this point had practically no knowledge of Greek philosophy beyond the logic of Aristotle. For John of Salisbury, Aristotle was already "the Philosopher"; he maintained his pre-eminence in the thirteenth century. Plato received little attention: the *Meno* and the *Phaedo,* translated in Sicily about the middle of the twelfth century, apparently did not exert any great influence. This does not, however, exclude an indirect, multiform, and powerful influence from Platonism. But an intense labor of Aristotelian translation lasted for more than a century and spanned the period between the activity of two men: Gundissalinus, archdeacon of Segovia (who died in 1151), and William of Moerbeke (who died in 1286). William, who was a Dominican and collaborator of St. Thomas, translated not only the works of Aristotle and his ancient commentators but also the *Elements of Theology* and other works of Proclus. He proceeded directly from Greek into Latin, while Gundissalinus and the other translators of Toledo worked with Arabic versions. Aristotle arrived therefore, not alone, but in the company of miscellaneous works: his Moslem disciples and Jewish philosophers profoundly influenced by Neoplatonism were also translated; a *Theologia* and a *De causis* derived, via Arabic and even Syriac, from the *Enneades* of Plotinus and the *Theology* of Proclus were attributed to Aristotle. (The *De causis* as well as a pseudo-Hermetic *Liber XXIV philosophorum* had already been used by Alain de Lille). Today the philosophical syncretism developed in the East is seen as a "decisive factor in the evolution of medieval thought." Before its advent in the West, Peripateticism had not only passed through the minds of Moslems or Jews, where it received Neoplatonic accretions, but the Arabic world had received the heritage of antiquity from Syriac schools whose masters were Christians. The complexity of these problems must at least be indicated in order to see the place of the thirteenth-century scholastics in the transmission of Greek philosophy throughout the Mediterranean world.

At the end of this astonishing *translatio studii,* these men discovered the *Physics* and the *Metaphysics* of Aristotle, the *Ethics* as well as the *Politics.* This discovery, which Paris made after 1200, fifty years later than Toledo, is a continuation of the renaissance that we have seen animating the twelfth century. I am well aware that, traditionally, the application of this word to the thirteenth century is rejected. This expression nevertheless makes it possible to recapture something of the vitality and activity of the period, and enables us to understand the former significance of disciplines which have today lost their attractiveness. If dialectic was able to create enthusiasm, to possess all the charm of a profane novelty, to enter into conflict with tradition, with the sacred, would this not be equally true of the Peripatetic construction of the world? When reduced to logic, philosophy never constituted more than an instrument; the handling of it could sometimes be delicate in matters of faith, but religious problems constituted virtually the sole subjects for reasoning. With the new translations, the perspective changed: philosophy was seen as a physics and a metaphysics, a doctrine of the world and even of God, apparently complete and rationally linked together. The works of the Philosopher and his followers were "read" to learn not only the art of reasoning but also the nature of things, while the nature of man became the rule for his conduct. Two books, three books, and then finally the whole of the *Nicomachean Ethics,* with a selection from the Greek commentaries, were an indication of what constituted a philosophical morality, a natural wisdom.

Reason appeared with a systematic content, independent of Christianity, or rather thrust into a non-Christian world: the discovery of nature, M.-D. Chenu notes, was accomplished more by Aristotle than by reason. In this atmosphere of discovery, minds continued to move in a realm of authors, but some of them, "the philosophers," were new. Here then "Renaissance means awakening, fervor, intoxication; but also recourse to a model already made, light that is borrowed—in short, imitation." In the order of thought, this situation allowed of a paradox, which did not escape St. Albert the Great: "All of the Peripatetics," he pointed out, "agree that what Aristotle said is true. They say that by displaying in him the supreme perfection of the human intellect, this man was ordained by nature as a model of truth. Nevertheless they expound him in different ways, according to the nature of their own thought." A source of disagreement for Greek commentators and modern historians, how could the Aristotelian texts be anything else for medieval men, who received them, with an assortment of ancient and Arabic interpretations, separately and from different sources? The Aristotelian invasion of the thirteenth century is too complex a phenomenon to attempt to distinguish here schematically except in two different waves: both bearing Aristotle with only one principal interpreter—Avicenna in the first case, Averroës in the second. Of the two Arabic thinkers, however, it was Avicenna who arrived first.[2]

The essential part of Aristotle's work—the *Logic,* the *Metaphysics,* the *Physics,* and a treatise *On the Soul*—was translated in the middle of the twelfth century in Toledo. Although we cannot expound the entire system

[2] Here are some dates relative to Arabic thinkers: Alkindi died in 873, Al-Farabi in 950, Avicenna (Ibn Sina) in 1037, Algazel (Al Gazali) about 1111: these men lived in the East. Averroës (Ibn Roschd) was born in Cordova in 1126 and died in 1198. The principal figures in Jewish philosophy are Isaac Israeli, who lived in Egypt between 845 and 940; Ibn Gabirol (the Avicebron of the Latins) flourished in Spain about 1021-58; Moses Maimonides, born in Cordova in 1135, lived in Morocco, Palestine, and Egypt, where he died in 1204.

of Arabic philosophy, let us at least recall its attitude on an Aristotelian obscurity, as a result of which it will be possible to see the place of the work of Western Christians in a long tradition of commentaries and speculations. We will consider only authors known to the Latin world at the beginning of the thirteenth century. As a result of the experience of history, few Aristotelian texts would seem to be more difficult to clarify or more fertile of interpretations than *De anima* III, 5: in order to explain knowledge, the Philosopher tells us, it is necessary to posit "an intellect fit to become all things and an intellect capable of producing all things." The second of these two intellects is "separated," "unmoved," "unmixed," "act by essence," "immortal and eternal," and acts on intelligible objects as light on color. It is possible to ask, as some still ask today, if this intellect in Aristotle's thought is not God or perhaps a supersensible being inferior to God (Ross). Commentators working on this problem prior to 1200 had added not a little complication and confusion, beginning with Alexander of Aphrodisias, whose doctrine was the point of departure for Arabic speculation on the subject of the intellect. From works often more closely related to a text than to the things it deals with, let us isolate a dominant tradition of thought: from the time of Alkindi, the active intellect of Alexander becomes an "Intelligence," that is to say, a substance separated from the sensible, distinct from the soul, but inferior to God. Al-Farabi places it in an intermediate position: in the lowest rank of a hierarchy of Intelligences, each of which moves one of the celestial spheres; God, being distinct from the mover of the first heaven, is above the series: there is no attempt to identify with Him the intellect that acts on human souls. Consequently, the soul ceases to derive all of its knowledge from the sensible; it can, in certain cases, unite itself with the separated Intelligence: then a man becomes a "prophet."

These themes are found again in Avicenna, whose fame caused his predecessors to be forgotten. He too

unites the theory of the intellect with the construction
of the astronomical world, and superimposes on the
abstraction another method of knowing that is sacred in
character. Avicennianism is, in effect, a kind of cosmogony,
in which all other beings emanate from the necessary
Being: since they themselves are pure possibilities, their
essences receive *existence* as an accident, but it is a necessary existence which, by means of *natural* generosity, the
"First Being" communicates to them. This discussion of
the "problem of existence," can be attributed to the conflict between a "theology of the Old Testament" and the
emanationism of Proclus (Gilson). From the "First" then
comes the first Intelligence, which in turn generates the
second Intelligence, the soul and body of the first sphere.
Descending through the various degrees, one comes to the
Intelligence of the moon, which is not the source of the
soul or body of a sphere, but of a last Intelligence, the
souls of men and the four elements. This *"active* Intelligence" engenders all the forms—intelligibility in thought
as well as health in the body. "The fragment of a sphere
that has not come into existence," the relationship between
the individual, body and soul, and the active Intellect, is
of the same order as that which exists between each
celestial sphere and the Intelligence from which it proceeds. The analysis of knowledge is related to a cosmic
perspective. Just as the physician prepares the body for
the reception of health, the elaboration of the data of
sense perception prepares thought for the reception of the
intelligible. Let us imagine a soul that effortlessly turns
itself toward the Intelligence: its state will constitute a
form of prophecy.

The Christian Middle Ages also knew Avicenna through
the exposition of Algazel, a theologian opposed to the
philosophers: he calls the active Intellect the distributor
of forms—*dator formarum*—a name that conforms perfectly to its physical function. The same author skillfully
reconsiders the theme of prophecy as union with the
separated Intelligence: in a hierarchical world in which

no degree can be lacking, prophecy is necessary in order to represent knowledge which frees itself from the senses. This doctrine will awaken some unforseen echoes among the Christian readers of Moslem thinkers.

The influence of this wave of Aristotelianism in the West was operative in a system of "authors." The philosophers who had just been translated merely represented some new texts. But since authors exemplifying the religious tradition had already been established before the arrival of the new works, there was an immediate attempt to make both live side by side in the same mind. Even as late as the fifteenth century, the *De anima* of William of Vaurouillon will undertake to unite the analysis of the mind "according to the philosophers," with that "according to the theologians." If their original sense is not too closely adhered to, formulas with diverse origins can be made to harmonize in some common resonance. Within the confines of the twelfth and thirteenth centuries, a number of works illustrate this process, rather more an association of ideas than a work of synthesis, but with a consciousness of the difficulties to be resolved—the *De anima* of Gundissalinus, for example, and a *De causis primis et secundis,* which has been attributed to him. According to his prologue, the author of the *De anima* sought to bring together all that he found reasonable in the sayings of the philosophers relative to the soul. At the end of this work, he states that he has avoided speculation on man after the Resurrection, since the philosophers have said nothing about this. In Gundissalinus's compendium, various extracts from Avicenna present the theory of the Intellect; the Jewish philosopher Ibn Gabirol is also represented, as is Boethius; there is something of the tradition of St. Augustine; one seems to hear an echo of St. Bernard. The treatise is, in effect, concerned with the problem of a knowledge of the intelligible without intermediary. Boethius relates it to the *intelligentia,* which is extremely rare among men; it is also possible to speak of *sapientia,* thinking of *sapere,* "to taste"; this intelligence or wisdom has a mystical savor: we attain it only rarely, and then briefly—*rara hora et parva mora*—when we are, as it were, lifted up—*raptim*—to the point of sensing something of God. The Christian mystic here takes the place of the Moslem prophet. But in addition, after having reproduced the Avicennian doctrine of the separated Intellect, the soul is said to be illuminated by God, the "Sun of Justice, the Father of light." This syncretism, Gilson notes, foreshadows that of Peter of Spain, the author of a *Scientia de anima,* or of Roger Bacon or Albert the Great. With the *De fluxu entis* or *De causis primis et secundis,* the mingling becomes more complex, and abundant use is made of John the Scot. This work, too, is made up of bits and pieces; the compiler's method of proof by the invocation of authors seems invincible to him. This method of marshaling authorities is called the *modus authenticus.* An extraordinary assemblage of texts is the result. It has been called Neoplatonic, but in this case it is something very entangled, since Augustine, Gregory of Nyssa, Pseudo-Denis, Erigena, the *De causis,* and Avicenna, under whose name the book was presented, are all represented. One can see the confused state of the material available for speculative work, surely something entirely different from the classical system of Aristotle.

In Paris during the first years of the thirteenth century, the historian perceives a multiplicity of intellectual currents. In the first place, there is instruction in theology that continues the tradition of Peter Lombard by glosses, commentaries on the *Sentences,* or *summae* that in themselves are indicative of the development of philosophical knowledge. In the second place, there is the influence of the Eastern theological themes that appear in the theses—some of them inspired by Erigena—condemned in 1241. Finally, there is the diffusion of Aristotelianism, a word which, as we have indicated, covers a multitude of complexities, but of whose influences at least two must be mentioned—Avicenna and Alexander of Aphrodisias, partially translated from the Arabic. What connection can be established between these two currents and the very incompletely understood "pantheistic" doctrines of Amaury (Amalric) of Bena and David of Dinant? Whatever may be the origin and the meaning of their formulas, the condemnations that strike them in 1210 and 1215 indicate a ferment that the authorities evidently associated with the Aristotelian translations and commentaries. Aristotle's works —with the exception of his *Logic*—were also condemned. The regulations for the University approved by Innocent III's legate Robert of Courson in 1215, prescribe that "neither the books of Aristotle on metaphysics and natural philosophy, nor the *summae* that treat of them, nor the teaching of David of Dinant, nor of Amaury the heretic, nor of Maurice of Spain are to be read." [3] Let us leave Erigena, Amaury, and David aside, and Maurice of Spain, too, who is still a mystery to us despite many hypotheses. We can verify a diffusion of the *Physics* and *Metaphysics* of Aristotle, and as for the "*summae*" and "commentaries," those of Al-Farabi and Avicenna can be mentioned.

The reaction of the Church was the consequence of a predetermined conception of the role of the University. Gregory IX—a man who, however, had just imposed studies on the Franciscan Order—takes up once more the brutal comparison of Peter Damian: "The young girl taken from the enemy, after her hair is shaven and her nails cut, is united with an Israelite. She must not dominate him, but rather obey him as a subject. In this virile way, the theological intellect must dominate all disciplines. . . ." Three years later, in 1231, doubtlessly to convert this metaphor of the captive woman into reality, the same pope will consider purging the natural philosophy of Aristotle of its errors. But there was to be no such revision; Aristotle takes up residence in Paris. The Papacy, however, had formulated its point of view; the other sciences

---

[3] *Non legantur libri Aristotelis de metaphysica et de naturali philosophia, nec summae de eisdem aut de doctrina magistri David de Dinant, aut Almauri haeretici aut Mauricii hispani.*

which were taught in the faculty of arts ought to *serve* theology, which is, it is recalled, wisdom founded on Scripture—*sapientia sacrae paginae*. We encounter the famous theme: *philosophia ancilla theologiae*. If the thirteenth century transformed an apparently rebellious philosophy into the servant of theology, it was not by resorting to force but rather by a subtle art, exercised, as we shall see, with a variety of effects.

Guillaume d'Auvergne, a master in theology at Paris and bishop of that city from 1228, is a valuable witness for the Aristotelian invasion. He was acquainted with Alexander of Aphrodisias, who, when confronted with the separated and divine *active intellect,* conceived of a *passive intellect* that corresponded to it, the *material intellect,* as a simple form for the body—a "disposition," our theologian says, an "accident" of corporeal substance. This "error," this "folly," must be discussed because of the authority that so renowned a commentator on the Philosopher has for weak minds; without discussion men "avail" themselves of all the opinions of such an author. Alexander, moreover, is but one of Guillaume's adversaries; he attacks an entire class: *philosophi maxime peripatetici, id est sequaces Aristotelis et qui famosiores fuerunt de gente Arabum in disciplinis Aristotelis.* He is concerned with philosophers, especially Peripatetics—that is, disciples of Aristotle and of those Arabs, such as Avicenna, who were most celebrated. To distinguish the uncreated from the created, our theologian knows how to utilize the Avicennian doctrine of essence and existence, but he juxtaposes the true God to the Principle of a necessary *natural* emanation, out of which *immediately only one* creature can arise, and rejects the equation of the two: the Creator is almighty and absolutely free. The Intelligences and the souls of the spheres fare no better: Guillaume, not without humor, compares the celestial souls to the horses and asses that make the mills of men go round; as for the ten Intelligences of Avicenna, the Christian admits the angels, but he knows that they are more numerous. For Avicenna, creation is accomplished by degrees: the active Intelligence constitutes the principle from which our souls emanate, as well as the end to which they must return. The separated intellect takes the place of the true God. Here again is that radical requirement used by Hugh of Saint-Victor in his rejection of the "theophanies" of Erigena: God is *immediately* our beginning and our end. The world of the Christian scholastic, like that of Avicenna, possesses a hierarchical structure: pure intelligences exist between man and God; angels have their fixed place in medieval thought, they can even be given an astronomical office. The human soul, however, still enjoys a direct relationship with its Creator. Between ourselves and God, no other nature is interposed; St. Augustine had expressed this fundamental concept: *nulla natura interposita*. And in addition, the Creator had counted the generations, in a world which was temporally finite; Christians will leave to philosophers their world without beginning, their generations without end.

Guillaume d'Auvergne charges Avicenna with still other errors. If individualization results from matter, how can souls be personally immortal? This same interpretation of the individual leads to the idea that the singular is unintelligible, just like the matter from which it proceeds. Here again we find ourselves in opposition to the faith according to which our end consists in knowing God, who is singular, in the highest degree—*cum enim creator singularissimus sit*. We encounter here problems which, in 1270 and 1277, theologians will juxtapose to "Averroism" and which will still dominate the polemic of Duns Scotus against "the philosophers" at the beginning of the fourteenth century. Several generations will think in reaction against Arabic Aristotelianism, but not without utilizing its philosophical techniques in theology and adjusting certain of its doctrines to the tradition of sacred teaching. Thus it is that Guillaume d'Auvergne, in his explanation of human knowledge, orients himself toward one of these formulas of balance. Let us sketch his doctrine, extremely complex and difficult to comprehend: the Christian man, he thinks, does not need to receive anything from an active Intelligence; but it is necessary to explain how his soul *receives* intelligibles. There is, in effect, in his essence a substratum of passivity: our theologian keeps "the intellect fit to become all things," the *material intellect.* How can the problem of knowledge be formulated in terms of this passive mind? By following Plato, it could be admitted that it submits to the action of intelligibles; but for medieval men, the Platonic Ideas were identified with universals—that is, genera and species. Here the problem is related to singulars: this man or that other one; man in general is not endowed with any efficacious reality. When Platonism becomes inconceivable, Aristotle's solution remains; as Guillaume says, the Philosopher admits an active Intelligence, filled with intelligibles, the form from which forms flow, *forma formiflua,* knowledge the maker of knowledge, *scientia scientifica*—this is the separated intellect which acts on our material intellect. This Intelligence filled with forms, *intelligentia plena formis,* takes us back to Avicenna, who was perhaps inspired on this point by Porphyry. The complexity of the intellectual situation is apparent: Plato's opponent is an Aristotle charged with Neoplatonism. What will now constitute "the Christian doctrine, necessarily true in all things, absolutely free from all error"? Guillaume shows us that our soul is placed, as it were, on the horizon between two worlds—on the one side, the sensible world; on the other, an intelligible world which is one with the Creator himself. The Old and New Testaments come to the support of this last idea: Ecclesiastes exalts the Word of God as the source of wisdom, the Gospel of John calls Him the true light which enlightens all men. By these texts, the God of tradition offers himself for the role of "the intellect capable of producing all things," which, according to Aristotle, acts "like light." We have no text from Guillaume which explicitly says that God is our active intellect. Roger Bacon

relates that the bishop of Paris condemned the opinion
of those who put this intellect in the soul—*intellectus
agens non potest esse pars animae*. That "the active intellect cannot be part of the soul"—or as we would say,
one of its faculties—is a thesis and formula of capital
importance. If Christians wished to use this philosophical
term and sought the object to which it could be applied,
it would have to be to God himself. We will find this theme
of God as the active intellect again in Robert Grosseteste,
Roger Bacon, and others. In this context, Gilson speaks of
"Avicennian Augustinianism": Avicenna's texts on the separated Intelligence of the soul meet with those of Augustine
on the Word illuminator, and become the objects of new
interest; the theologians' fidelity to Augustine takes on a
philosophical interpretation.

About 1230 the efforts to translate Averroës were cen-
tered in the Italian court of the Emperor Frederick II.
Coming somewhat later than Avicenna, the influence of
Averroës led not only to the more or less free utilization
of his interpretation of Aristotle by individual authors, but
to the formation of an Averroistic school, similar to that
of the fourteenth and fifteenth centuries, which links the
Paduans of the Renaissance—more or less unbelieving men
obstinately holding to the natural philosophy of Aristotle
—with thirteenth-century Parisian masters in arts. The
later Averroists considered Siger de Brabant as a founder;
his teaching, along with that of Boethius of Dacia, was included in the condemnation of 1277—a decisive moment,
in Gilson's judgment, in the history of scholasticism. Before
we approach the problems raised for twentieth-century
historians by the epithet "Averroistic" in application to
this teaching, we must consider Averroës himself.

Averroës reproaches Avicenna for having listened to
Islamic theologians and mingling their ideas with his
metaphysics; Duns Scotus will remember this remark. The
Cordovan philosopher, leaving to religion the idea of an
existence superimposed on merely possible essences, and
seeing no sense in discussing even the nontemporal origin

of the world given its eternal structure, desires to be solely a philosopher by being the Commentator of the Philosopher, and this will be his title. Does not one read in his works that nature displays for us in Aristotle, as in a model, the ultimate in human perfection, given to us by Providence that we might know all that can be known? Philosophy cannot be more closely identified with a text. As presented by Averroës, Aristotle's writings form a corpus to be accepted or rejected as a whole—the system, as it were, of written reason. For men who arrive at this state of mind, nothing remains to be done but to accept the theses of the Philosopher, in the sense of the Commentator. The risk is evident: philosophical speculation could be reduced to an Aristotelian commentary. But an advantage is equally possible: having experienced the force with which the writings of the Philosopher as explained by the Commentator reject some of the theses of faith, some theologians will know that philosophy cannot be made to say what one might like it to say (Gilson).

In fact, the doctrines that Guillaume d'Auvergne denounced in Avicenna are also found in Averroës. Moreover, one of the interpretations peculiar to the Commentator, the most remarkable theory in Latin Averroism, is an analysis of the intellect incompatible with Revelation. Let us take up the problem of Alexander of Aphrodisias again: the active intellect is separated, leaving for man only the material intellect, the corporeal form that has no other destiny than that of the body for which it is the form. For Averroës the reasons that necessitate the separation of the active intellect are valid for the material intellect—the pure receptivity of intelligibles in the contact of the active intellect with the imagination that alone is corporeal; the intellect is both incorruptible and one for all men. The multiplicity of bodies to which it is joined remains outside of it. The intellect, even the passive intellect, is immortal, but not individually immortal; the doctrine implies only the eternity of the human species. In this view of the unity of the intellect—*de unitate intellectus*—the negation of individual survival proceeds not from any joining of the understanding and the body, but from the radical distinction between them. Some theologians were unable to reconcile themselves to this position; Avicenna, on the other hand, with his multiple passive intellects, left open the possibility of personal immortality. If God takes the place of a subaltern Intelligence as the principle of illumination in this life and the next, Christians can accept Avicenna's theory of the intellect; Thomas Aquinas, who rejects it, does say, however, that it is preferable to the position of Averroës.

How was it possible for masters in the faculty of arts in a Christian institution, during a century of common faith, to teach the theses condemned in 1270: the unity of the intellect, for example, or the ascendency of necessity over will, or the eternity of the world, or God's ignorance of all that is not a part of him? We do not know if any master taught these and certain other Averroistic propositions. Not all of the 219 theses proscribed in 1277 by the bishop of Paris, Etienne Tempier, with the approbation of Pope John XXI, were derived from Averroës; some came from Avicennianism and even Thomism. If the contemporary writings of St. Bonaventure, St. Thomas, St. Albert the Great, and Giles of Rome indicate a certain alarm with respect to the teaching of famous masters in philosophy —magistri qui in philosophia majores reputantur—the known work of the most celebrated among them, Siger de Brabant, does not completely clarify the significance of "Latin Averroism." Even this expression, justified in the interpretation of Mandonnet, is contestable after the work of Van Steenberghen, who speaks of an "integral Aristotelianism," and elsewhere of a "Neoplatonic Aristotelianism." It does not seem that we are confronted with a system of reason completely opposed to the system of faith, but rather with a series of questions for which variously shaded answers were given. The sources are complex: Siger sometimes follows Avicenna instead of Averroës; the influence of Proclus seems to be important;

when, for example, the distinction between essence and existence is once rejected in the spirit of Averroës and Aristotle, it is necessary to ask again if first causality is operative only in the order of movement, on the level that the Commentator maintains. With respect to the relationship between the intellect and the human composite, where he follows Averroës, who was himself influenced by Plotinus, and rejects the solutions of Albert and of Thomas, whom he considered eminent philosophers —*praecipui viri in philosophia*—Siger remarks: "Here, we seek only the direction the philosophers tend to take, Aristotle in particular, even if it is discovered that the Philosopher thinks something that is not true, concerning the subject of the soul, where Revelation has transmitted something to us that we cannot conclude from natural reason. Therefore, in this case, we do not have to consider the miracles of God, since we treat naturally of natural things." Teaching in a faculty of arts, not of theology, Siger is true to his calling and to that alone: to philosophize by explaining the Philosopher. He sometimes arrives at a philosophically irrefutable conclusion that is opposed to religious dogma; he does not qualify it as truth since in faith, he says, speaks "the truth that cannot lie." Theologians who will not accept this intellectual position will have to refute "the philosophers" by an effort that we must indeed call philosophical: by rationally proving the opposite of their theses or at least demonstrating that they were not truly founded on reason.

The "Averroism" of Siger de Brabant or of Boethius of Dacia is apparently simply the fact that masters in arts, working in their sphere and holding to it without questioning the truth of faith, wished to be philosophers and nothing more. It is not without interest to note here that one reads among the propositions condemned in 1277: *Quod non est excellentior status quam vacare philosophiae. Quod sapientes sunt philosophi tantum*—"There is no more noble state than to occupy oneself with philosophy. Only philosophers are wise." The title of Boethius of Dacia's

De summo bono sive de vita philosophi indicates its central idea: the highest good and the life of the philosopher are one and the same. In a precise and beautiful style, this short treatise expounds, without envisioning anything beyond, the ideal of a purely natural wisdom. Here we find not only metaphysical theses in conflict with dogma, but a conception of life according to a nature that has no recourse to grace. One of the theses condemned in 1277 denies that to humble oneself is a virtuous act. One question of Siger takes up the Aristotelian notion of magnanimity, without attempting, as Albert the Great or Thomas Aquinas had done, to reconcile it with the theology of humility. The introduction of the *Nicomachean Ethics* into medieval Christendom raised some problems that the fourteenth-century Augustinian Hugolino of Orvieto will declare unsolvable when he says that the Philosopher's magnanimity is the pride of the Pharisee, a suggestion that makes one think of Luther.

For Mandonnet, "Latin Averroism bears witness to the attractive power exerted by ancient thought as it penetrated the soul of medieval Europe. It was inevitable that a certain number of intellectuals would submit to it without reservation." Even if these last two words are contestable, and if the complex and varied history of the "Averroists" from the thirteenth century to the sixteenth century remains to be written, the Aristotelian invasion can be seen as part of a renaissance movement. For, whatever opinion one may have of his philosophy, Aristotle remains a classical author, Avicenna is permeated with Neoplatonism, and of Averroës it has been said that he was the most Greek of the Arabic philosophers. There is no doubt that under such influences medieval Latin became a purely technical language, without concern for form, while education became completely abstract. But this cultural impoverishment had its compensations. Scholasticism was not in any sense a narrow, closed school. The Christians of the West endlessly referred to the speculations of the Moslems and Jews of Asia Minor and

Spain; and they did so to such an extent that our ignorance of Avicenna or Maimonides can prevent us from understanding Thomas Aquinas or Duns Scotus. Let us not forget either the breadth of the medieval intellectual horizon or the cultural communication of these scholastics with very diverse races, which made the classical language of Aristotelianism the common intellectual language of the period. In this relationship to the ancient world, the medieval man saw a problem essential to him; when considering the virtues of the philosophers, Alcuin saw no difference between them and Christians except for faith and baptism; for the men of the thirteenth century this distinction remained the basis of all others—that is, they considered the philosophy they had just received as a construction of the world and an organization of life which dispensed with the Christian God and his grace. Aristotle was man simply as man, as pure natural reason. The idea of nature became the foundation of a mental universe: Siger de Brabant wanted "to treat all things naturally"; Boethius of Dacia gave this definition of philosophy: "I call a philosopher any man who, living according to the true order of nature, has acquired the best and ultimate end of human life."

Attitudes of this kind explain why, in the first years of the fourteenth century, the theologian Duns Scotus went to great lengths to prove that some sort of revelation was necessary to determine the end of man and to put him on the road that leads there. To express the nature of the problem, he writes: "In this question, there seems to be a controversy between philosophers and theologians. The philosophers posit in effect the perfection of nature and deny the perfection of the supernatural. But the theologians *know what is lacking in nature* and consequently the necessity for grace and supernatural perfections." Logically, a man who defines himself as a nature integrated in the natural order of a harmonious world admits the sufficiency of this nature; such is the sense of the Aristotelian maxim that nature is not deficient in what is necessary

—*natura non deficit in necessariis*. On the other hand, the believer recalls a passage in St. Augustine: "The object of our faith is such that we can neither be ignorant of it, nor know it through our own powers." By placing man in this paradoxical situation, the theologians say to the philosophers that they merely recognize the essential deficiency of nature. *Cognoscunt vero defectum naturae*— with these remarks made at the end of the thirteenth century, Duns Scotus foreshadows Pascal. But the position that he will take does not in any way suggest Jansenism, in fact quite the contrary is true.

But let us not pass so quickly, with Scotus, into the fourteenth century. As early as the twelfth century, M.-D. Chenu has found, together with the concept of cosmic values and the notion of a microcosm, an idea of the human being as a "nature in Nature." With its natural philosophy and its "cosmic morality," the Aristotelianism of the thirteenth century is a continuation of this movement; the reaction of 1277 strikes against a "polymorphous naturalism." In a situation such as this, where man acquires consciousness of himself by receiving the heritage of the ancients, and as a part of this heritage, the natural philosophy of Aristotle, humanism is formulated in terms of naturalism, and the conflict of the human with the divine is defined as the opposition between nature and grace. This opposition was known to the century we have studied. The subsequent conflict between nascent modern science and Aristotelian physics, then incorporated in the teaching of the theologians and defended by them, must not make us forget that, for the thirteenth century, the world "of the philosophers," in which natural man was defined, was opaque rather than transparent with respect to the faith that sought in it a sign of its God. Whoever has not grasped this possibility of antagonism cannot understand the medieval attempts at a balance, the scholastic formulas of harmony.

Chapter IV

THE INTELLECTUAL DIVERSITY OF THE THIRTEENTH CENTURY:
Robert Grosseteste and Roger Bacon, St. Bonaventure, St. Thomas and His Time, Movements Outside of Thomism

Today the thirteenth century is seen as the century of St. Thomas. The fortunes of Thomism in the twentieth century, however, must not deceive the historian studying the Middle Ages. The same age, remarkable for its speculative fecundity, knew of other approaches to doctrine that also produced masterpieces; an understanding of Thomas Aquinas, the man of a century, and of his teaching, cannot but lead one to the knowledge of other men and other speculative systems that answered the same historical situation. Too often Thomism has been thought of in the abstract. It is necessary to picture St. Thomas *in his time* and to recall the intellectual diversity of that age. We have already noted several characteristics of Latin Aver-

roism; something must now be said of the Oxonian masters
Robert Grosseteste and Roger Bacon, of the Franciscan
school of Paris which culminated in St. Bonaventure, and
finally of some thinkers who, after St. Thomas, flourished
outside of Thomism.

Oxford, in the thirteenth century, continued the twelfth-
century tradition of Chartres in its quest for an encyclopedic culture and in its attachment to the disciplines of
the *quadrivium* as renovated by contact with the Arabs.
The followers of Adelard of Bath secured for England
a scientific erudition such as was not to be found on the
Continent in the early years of the thirteenth century.
We can confine our attention to a typical effort of method-
ical knowledge: the optics or *Perspective* of Alhazen (965-
1039), as remarkable for its theory of light as for its
analysis of perception. This work of an Islamic mathematician, translated about 1200, orients the reader toward
an intellectual climate that is quite different from the
Physics of Aristotle. Those who appreciated it seem to us
to be turned toward the future development of science.
But let us not detach them from the age in which they
lived.

The intellectual activity of Robert Grosseteste,[1] a contemporary of Guillaume d'Auvergne, was extremely diver-
sified. Roger Bacon, his pupil, extols his knowledge of
languages, which enabled him to understand both the
Fathers and the philosophers; he did, in fact, complete
or revise earlier translations from the Greek, including
the *Nichomachean Ethics*, the works of St. John Dama-
scene, and the writings of the Pseudo-Denis (or Pseudo-
Dionysius), at that time the object of general interest in
Paris. To this last he added a commentary; he also wrote
a commentary on Aristotle's *Posterior Analytics* that was
to be influential for a long time. But the concept of human
knowledge did not claim his attention exclusively.

[1] Robert Grosseteste, born in 1175 in Suffolk, was first a master
and then chancellor at the University of Oxford. A friend of
the Franciscans, he became bishop of Lincoln in 1235 and died
in 1253.

With respect to the object of theology, Grosseteste proposes a remarkable theory; by inviting all to be *one* in Him, the Christ of St. John reveals to us the contents of the wisdom which consists in knowing the unity that He himself encompasses: the substantial unity of the Father with the Son and the Holy Spirit; the unity of the human and divine natures united, that unity by which all Christians are one, *unus*, in Christ; the unity of the Trinitarian God with intellects renewed in His image. From this point of view, the theologian can consider in turn the Trinity and what makes it one; the incarnate Word and his body, the Church; and finally what makes man godlike in form and similar to the Trinity. The theological horizon extends beyond humanity: all creatures belong to this wisdom in as much as they flow out from this unity and return to it—*Creaturae etiam omnes in quantum ab hoc uno fluunt et in hoc unum recurrunt ad istam pertinent sapientiam.* Not to point out this "Christo-centrism" would be to neglect one aspect of the state of mind of the Middle Ages. In the idea of the whole Christ—*Christus integer*—incorporating the Church and all things within himself, it is possible to find a principle for viewing the world with the eyes of faith.

The atmosphere in which Grosseteste lived appears once again in his commentary on the *Posterior Analytics*—in his explanation, for example, of the celebrated formula "one less sense, one less science." All knowledge, he says, can exist without recourse to the senses; the knowledge God possesses of all things is proof of this. The same is true of Intelligences—that is to say, of Angels—for although these beings have no senses, they still receive the irradiation of divine light. Our soul itself, provided it is not dulled by the body, can similarly receive a perfect knowledge in its superior part, which Grosseteste calls the "intelligence." This principle stated, our author explains how a soul, preoccupied with the body, and as it were asleep, can awaken itself by sensations and arrive at the universal. In fact, reason, drowsy in us, acts only after stimulation by the senses. This is because every soul gazes at what it loves; oriented by sin toward the body and its delights, it turns away from the intelligible light so long as the least reflection on the sensible does not make it seek this light that corresponds to its nature—a light it will rediscover in proportion to its detachment: only the pure of heart shall see God. The necessity of beginning with the senses, as posited by Aristotle, is explained by the present state of mankind, fallen with Adam and re-ascending toward beatitude. In his doctrine of sensation and again in the related idea of illumination, the influence of St. Augustine can be recognized. But Grosseteste's *De veritate* is above all reminiscent of St. Anselm. These are the data of the problem: Christ said: "I am the way, *the* truth, and the life"; but he also said: the Spirit "will teach you *all* truth." How can the unity of truth be reconciled with the multiplicity of truths? To give an answer, let us begin with human language; by means of intellection and conception, the elements of an inner discourse, we come to the notion of the divine Word, the discourse of the Father—*sermo Patris:* everything is absolutely what this discourse says. The Word, as he has revealed it, constitutes *the* Truth. Things appear true in as much as they conform to the eternal word: these constitute the multiple truths. In all cases, to use Anselm's terminology, truth consists in a "rectitude"—"regulating," as it were, in the Creator (*rectitudo rectificans*); "regulated" in creatures (*rectitudo rectificata.* It is at this point that St. Augustine and illumination intervene: How could an intellect recognize the rectitude of a thing if it were to remain absolutely outside the rule which "rectifies" it? All created truth can only be seen in the light of the supreme truth: *omnis creata veritas non nisi in lumine veritatis summae conspicitur.* Although this text does not speak of the active intellect, one can accept Roger Bacon's testimony that Grosseteste identified this principle with God.

By comparing God to a light, a theory of knowledge is formulated; from a consideration of corporeal light, it is

possible to draw a cosmogony. Robert's *De luce* takes
light for corporeality itself, the first form that is united
with matter to constitute bodies: something without extension, from which, as soon as it is posited, there follows
the extension of matter—in itself also without extension—
in three dimensions. What then is the nature of light? To
multiply, to propagate, and to diffuse itself: give us a
point of light, and instantaneously we have a luminous
sphere. With this as a point of departure, Robert Grosseteste constructs a Universe consisting of a first sphere, then
nine celestial spheres, and finally four spheres correspond-
ing to the elements. This world seems strange to us; the
consequences of the deduction are of little interest for
us. But from the point of view of the history of thought,
the results of such efforts at imaginative physics are much
less important than the perception of the intellectual
values that are found enmeshed in them. In short, this
theory of light with its concern for dimensions, points,
and spheres, indicates a geometric point of view.

A treatise *On Lines, Angles, and Figures* tells us: "It is
extremely useful to consider lines, angles, and figures,
since without these things it is impossible to understand
natural philosophy." Views of this sort are applied to the
entire universe and to each of its parts, to movement, and
to operations on matter and on the senses themselves.
There follows an analysis of natural action, which must be
accomplished by means of lines, angles, and figures: if
the causes of natural effects were not given in geometric
forms, a demonstrative science of them would be impossible. *Omnes enim causae effectuum naturalum habent dari
per lineas, angulas et figuras. Aliter enim impossible est
sciri "propter quid" in illis.* Nature acts according to the
straight line, conforming to a principle of economy and
perfection, that is to say, it operates in the shortest and
best possible way—*natura operatur breviori et meliori
modo quo potest.* The same mathematician's aesthetics is
found in a treatise on the rainbow, which speaks of the
most precise, the most ordered, the shortest and best

method—*modus finitissimus, ordinatissimus, brevissimus et optimus*. Another work suggests that geometry holds the key for discovering natural causes: "These rules, roots, and fundamentals having been once acquired through the power of geometry, the man who carefully observes the things of nature can by following this path give causes for all natural effects"—*His igitur regulis et radicibus et fundamentis datis ex potestate geometriae, diligens inspector in rebus naturalibus potest dare causas omnium effectuum naturalium per hanc viam*. It was this recognition of the utility of geometry in natural philosophy that proved most interesting to Roger Bacon, even before the twentieth century singled it out as the most significant of Grosseteste's intuitions.

It is perhaps too much to say that Grosseteste was the first to treat "systematically of the role of experiment in scientific research" (Crombie). Without any doubt the commentary on the *Posterior Analytics* conceives of a method of discovering inductively principles from which it is possible to discover deductively the facts and the way to prove the validity of these premises. The problem of definition gives rise to the question of a valid "conceptualization" of data. A principle of economy forms the criterion for making a choice among what we would call hypotheses; all things being equal, the best demonstration is the one which requires the fewest presuppositions—*demonstratio dignior ex minoribus suppositionibus*. Elsewhere a principle of causal induction is formulated: things of the same nature produce the same effects—*res ejusdem naturae ejusdem operationis secundum naturam suam effectivae sunt*. As a follower of Grosseteste in this matter, Duns Scotus will speak of the nondemonstrative knowledge of the expert—*expertus, demonstratione carens, sciens*—founded on the certitude that since causes are not free —*causa non libera*—natures act uniformly and systematically—*uniformiter et ordinate*. But in this context it should be noted that to point out the elements of a logic of induction in the Middle Ages is not the same as finding the beginnings of scientific experiment linked with measurement.

This remark also applies to Grosseteste's Franciscan pupil Roger Bacon.[2] Since Descartes, two mental regimes are generally contrasted: the one scholastic, founded on Aristotelian logic; the other modern, deriving an art of thinking from mathematics. For Bacon, logic depends on mathematics: the heart of this discipline is the art of demonstrating, the subject of the *Posterior Analytics,* and it is only in mathematics that it is possible to know and to show clearly what principles and conclusions are, what constitutes a true demonstration. Let us understand by this a proof that moves a priori by means of a distinct idea: a demonstration by proper and necessary cause— *demonstratio per causam propriam et necessariam.* There is nothing like this in the other sciences when they reject the aid of mathematics: *Excluso mathematicae beneficio, tot sunt dubitationes, tot opiniones, tot errores.* (If the benefit of mathematics is refused, only so many doubts, so many opinions, so many errors result!) But let us suppose that mathematics is applied to each of the sciences: "It will be shown that the other sciences are not to be understood by means of the dialectical and sophistic arguments commonly used, but by mathematical demonstrations that come down into the truths and workings of the other sciences that they subject to their rule; outside of these demonstrations, it is impossible to understand, to unveil, to teach, or to learn sciences." This program could be realized only by formulating certain treatises for all the sciences—*Sed hoc nihil aliud esset, nisi constituere tractatus certos de omnibus scientiis.* If the mathematics of the thirteenth century seem feeble enough in our eyes, these

[2] Roger Bacon, born in England about 1214, may have studied at Oxford before he came to Paris prior to 1245. He returned to Oxford about 1247 and entered the Franciscan Order about 1257. He returned to Paris and was in correspondence with Pope Clement IV (1265-68). He wrote his last work in 1292.

Oxonians had none the less perceived the immense fecundity of this discipline as a principle of universal explanation and a way to certitude.

To us Roger Bacon, like the bishop of Lincoln, appears to be turned toward the future. This prophet of mathematicism thought of himself, however, as the repository of a tradition: that of his masters Grosseteste and Adam Marsh—another Oxonian Franciscan whom we scarcely know except through the allusions of Bacon—as well as of "all the ancient sages who have studied mathematics in order to know all things." Despite the strength of this heritage, the mind of Friar Roger is sufficiently vast and well stocked to be able to offer us a surprising variety. Let us first mention the philologist and the humanist. An essential theme of his *Opus majus* is the *necessitas linguarum;* when he speaks of the necessity of knowing languages, he has in mind Greek, Hebrew, Arabic, and Chaldean. And he holds that medieval Latins, by their ignorance of these languages, do not measure up to the ideal standard of learning. The same Bacon whose style seems lamentable to us, thinks that moral philosophy must make virtue loved through artful exposition: "by an elegant manner of writing," he says, "so that great delight may arise in the hearts of those who read"—*per elegantem modum scripturae, ut delectatio magna oriatur in cordibus eorum qui legunt.* Bacon was also an admirer of Seneca and had the *De ira* and the *De clementia* copied for the use of the pope; he corrected the text, pointing out the important passages for his illustrious recipient, and added extracts from the *De tranquillitate animi* and the *De beata vita.* The spirit of Alcuin and of Abelard is found in his exaltation of the ancients: "Nothing is better designed to invite us to live properly, we who are born and brought up in grace, than to see men deprived of grace attain the ineffable dignity of holiness of life."

Let us move from the ancient world to the Arabs. Bacon's work is full of their influence; his Avicennianism is patent. In his judgment, Avicenna is without peer among those who have expounded Aristotle, the greatest of those who have imitated him—*Avicenna vero praecipuus Aristotelis expositor et maximus imitator.* Different in this respect from the texts of Guillaume d'Auvergne and Robert Grosseteste—which, however, it quotes as authorities along with those of Adam Marsh—the doctrine of Friar Roger explicitly identifies the Word with the separated active intellect of Al-Farabi and Avicenna, the true interpreters of Aristotle. We are, in 1266-68, confronted by a traditionalist opposing a "modern" formula: "I point this out," he writes, "to prove the vanity of an extreme error, theological as well as philosophical. For all the moderns say that the intellect, which acts in our souls and illuminates them, is a part of the soul, so that there would be two parts to the soul: this active intellect and a possible intellect." Why does our Franciscan consider this error so grave and why is it so important to hold to the truth that it denies? Whether this active intellect is separated, or whether it is God himself, he tells us, is essential for my purpose, for I hold that all philosophy proceeds from a divine illumination. Let us quote the text: "Since it is necessary for the proof of my thesis to show that philosophy exists by means of divine influence, I wish to establish this in an efficacious way"—*Et quia istud est necessarium ad propositi persuasionem, ut ostendatur quod philosophia sit per influentiam divinae illuminationis, volo illud efficaciter probare.* Without going into the details of Bacon's theory of illumination, we can say that the idea of God as the active intellect places us in a world where all truth is from Christ, where philosophers, as inspired men, have received rather than acquired their knowledge, where philosophy does not differ radically from Revelation, where finally one can believe, with our Franciscan, that God revealed all things to the Patriarchs—by giving them lives that were so long that they could complete philosophy by means of experiences. Arabic Aristotelianism is utilized here to confirm the tradition of *one* perfect wisdom, contained in the Scriptures—*unam sapientiam esse perfectam, et*

hanc in sacris literis contineri. In Bacon we can find a
"theologism" as well as a mathematicism. *Sapientia est via
in salutem:* this wisdom, a way to salvation, is found in
Scripture. *Cum ergo sacra scriptura dat nobis hanc sapientiam, manifestum est quod hic veritas sit conclusa.* ("Since
Sacred Scripture gives us this wisdom, it is evident that
the truth is contained in it.") There is no greater possibility
of truth outside the sacred books than there are men who
can escape the divine admonition: "Who is not with me
is against me." Contrary to the expectations of the historian, a parallel principle leads our theologian not to reject
the profane sciences, but to cultivate them, and to fight
against the ignorance of his contemporaries. His theology,
in effect, insists on the radical unity of knowledge, a
principle, it would seem, of intellectual enthusiasm. Scripture contains all truth, but in a veiled state; it must be
unveiled (*explicare*). In this process, similar to unclench-
ing a fist, many disciplines seem to be necessary—not
only languages, mathematics, and perspective, but experimental science. *Scientia experimentalis:* an expression that
arrests the historian's attention!

Bacon does not, however, provide us with an *experimental method* for use in the several sciences, but with an
experimental science added to the other disciplines and
indicating to us a new "root" of wisdom. Experience has
a unique value; this can be seen even in mathematics. We
know that mathematical demonstrations "by proper and
necessary cause" guarantee this discipline "the whole truth
without error." Robert Grosseteste's student does not restrict himself to this point of view; he develops another
theme, "certitude exclusive of doubt," which in his eyes
seems different. Mathematics, he says, possesses "for all
things a perceptible example and a perceptible experience
of the fact that it traces figures and that it counts, so that
everything becomes clear to the senses: hence the impossibility of doubting." Other sciences lack "the experiences of constructing figures and of numeration, by
which all things must be affirmed." In mathematical

matters, where demonstration attains its full powers, it is possible to see that if the syllogism engenders knowledge, this is because it does not exclude a certain kind of experience: in effect, "it is essential to understand the meaning of a demonstration accompanied by experience, not the naked demonstration"—*intelligendum est si experientia comitetur, et non de nuda demonstratione.* Here the experience consists of *figuratio, numeratio.* In the mathematician's procedures, as a part of the statement and in the mathematical operation itself, Bacon perceives something besides logical connections.

Let us generalize: Without experience, nothing can be known in a satisfactory manner. There are, in fact, two modes of knowing: by argument and by experimentation. The argument arrives at a conclusion and forces us to concede its conclusion, but it does not *certify*, it does not banish doubt to the point that the mind rests in the sight of truth. For that, truth must be found by way of experience; "one sees, in fact, many men who argue about certain objects, but not having experience, they slight what they study, and by not avoiding what is detrimental, they do not obtain the gifts that are offered." The notion of experience appears in a certain psychological context: our Franciscan wants us to know in a binding and efficacious manner. There is an emotional aspect to certitude: like the soul resting in the contemplation of truth—*ut quiescat animus in intuitu veritatis.* Even when rigorous in itself, argumentation does not touch our soul. Bacon treats of the sciences only in view of that wisdom which, for the Christian, consists in the end in loving. And love expresses itself by its works. It is in this context that the value of experience is conceived. Then Bacon's double experimentalism, both physical and religious, becomes comprehensible: the *Opus majus* recognizes not only "human and philosophical experience," but also the experience of "interior illuminations." But let us leave the latter aside. In philosophy Bacon finds sciences that carefully draw their principles from experience, but they do not *certify* their conclusions by experiences. By applying mathematics to them, geometrical and arithmetical operations will be introduced; these do in fact constitute experiences, but they are universal, or as we would say, completely formal experiences. The task of experimental science and its first function is to find experiences that relate to the particular content of a problem, that achieve individual certitude. Its second "prerogative" consists in discovering, in the domain of the other sciences, truths other than their principles, which they cannot however attain as conclusions. "The third dignity of the art of experiment" no longer concerns its relationship to other disciplines, but all of its own wonderful works, from which Bacon expects great utility for the Christian commonwealth.

It is not difficult to point out some elements, disconcerting from our point of view, which enter into this science or art of experimenting—astrology, alchemy, and magic, for example. Let us add that even with reference to his own time, our friar does not seem an original experimenter. He did, however, see that reasoning does not take the place of either visual verification or manual operation: instruments interested him a great deal; Peter of Maricourt, a student of magnetism, no doubt taught him the importance of the *opus manuum,* of *industria manualis.* His feeling for mathematics, acquired from Grosseteste, and this penchant for manual dexterity form an important combination. At the same time, however, the Parisian masters abandoned themselves to abstract argumentation, to *nuda demonstratio.* Why then put too much of our modernity, of the twentieth century, into the mind of Roger Bacon? It is enough for this Oxonian Franciscan to exemplify, as opposed to the *moderni* of the thirteenth century, a consciousness of a cultural tradition that embraces more than the development of scholasticism.

Among these "moderns" unworthy of glory, Roger Bacon names his brother in religion Alexander of Hales—"a horse," writes the terrible Oxonian, "unable to carry his

Summa." Elsewhere, he adds, "it was not he, but others, who wrote it."

Twentieth-century historians familiar with the personal writings of Alexander, the first Franciscan master at Paris, know that the *Summa* is in fact a composite work, in which others, notably John of La Rochelle,[3] have had their part. The *Summa of Friar Alexander* acquaints us with a Franciscan university milieu, contemporary with Guillaume d'Auvergne, but quite differently oriented. We have seen Guillaume posit a soul completely passive before divine light: this bare possibility receives from on high a disposition to know, an infused *habitus*, in medieval terminology. Then as the Father engenders the Word, in God, "the intellective power impregnated, as it were, and made fertile by this disposition," engenders the sciences as actualities in itself. From a deep-seated passivity, we move to an activity which imitates the divine fecundity: in this manner of relating the soul, as an *image*, to the divine model, we have a mode of theological reasoning that "Alexander's" *Summa* utilizes to resolve, in a way which is opposed to "Avicennian Augustianism," the philosophical problem of the active intellect: How could God have created the soul in His image, without giving it the perfection of an activity with respect to what can be known? The senses see by an exterior light; the mind, more noble, possesses "a natural light." John of La Rochelle takes up the same thesis, by citing Scripture: "On us, Lord, the light of Thy Face is fixed." In Guillaume d'Auvergne, this biblical passage accompanied the idea of an illumination falling on a purely *possible* intellect; it is this same passage that is the basis, less than ten years later, for the notion of an active intellect as *part* of the soul: "interior light . . . imprinted on us by nature." This last idea will be found again in the great Franciscan master of Paris, St. Bona-

[3] Alexander of Hales, born in England shortly before 1186, was probably a master in theology by 1220-21, and was one of the first commentators on the *Sentences*. He became a Franciscan in 1236 and ceded his chair to John of La Rochelle; both men died in 1245.

venture,[4] who considered himself a continuator of his "master and father" Alexander of Hales.

In the thirteenth century, the active intellect and the possible intellect were the symbols of common data, but each thinker elaborated his concepts in his own way, according to the inclination of his reactions, according to his own interests, thus giving an individual orientation to a doctrine completely abstract in appearance. St. Bonaventure speaks the language of Aristotle, but without following the thought of his disciples. Let us ask, with him, what are the implications of the Peripatetic analysis of the soul? The philosophers have thought that an Intelligence ought to act on our soul: our faith does not allow this influence. Some Christians have said that God constituted our active intellect, our soul being reduced to the possible intellect: these individuals have not seen the problem that they had to resolve. Our God is truly "the true light, which enlightens all men." But, by proceeding from Him, human thought does not appear completely passive. On the contrary, "Although He constitutes the principal factor in the operation of every creature, God has however given to each one an active power so that it proceeds by its own proper operation. Furthermore, it must not be doubted that the human soul is not only given a possible intellect but an active intellect as well, both of which are part of the soul itself." Again in this instance, a theologian insists on the necessity of an active understanding. Since this correlative activity and passivity are parts of the same soul, we should not conceive of them as if they were not as united as the unity of a thinking being and its act requires. The active principle loses its transcendence: we witness the elimination of Avicennianism, and even of some concepts included in the very text of Aristotle, where we will find, on the one hand, a principle that makes everything and submits to nothing, and

[4] Giovanni Fidanza, surnamed Bonaventure, was born in 1221 in Bagnorea, near Viterbo. He entered the Order about 1238, taught at Paris from 1248 until 1255, and died in 1274.

on the other, a principle that submits to everything and makes nothing. For how could there be pure act in a creature and pure potency in a spiritual faculty?

An activity requiring assistance is joined to a passivity which does not act without spontaneity; the two intellects do not comprise all the conditions of knowledge—that is, certitude in judgment. For such is the nature of man's knowledge: *cognitio certitudinalis,* an expression characteristic of Bonaventure. The most classic question in which he explains that this characteristic of knowledge presupposes the presence in the mind of the "eternal reasons," the divine ideas, is one of his questions "on the knowledge of Christ." The fact of a God-man reunites the problems, or the mystery, of divine knowledge and human knowledge. Christ's knowledge as the Word extends to the infinity of possibles, knowable through the Ideas that are identical with the divine essence: an interior radiation of the uncreated Light. There is a connection between this doctrine of Ideas and that of the Word. Making use of Denis and Augustine, it deals with the knowledge of Christ as God; that of Christ as man, a problem with weighty implications, remains to be examined. In this extreme case of the union of the human understanding of finite being with divinity, the two manifest their harmony; there is no question of the infinite absorbing everything, nor of the supernatural obliterating the human.

Let us return to the human act of knowing with certitude. Such knowledge presupposes both immutability with respect to what one knows and infallibility in regard to the one who knows. But a *created* truth could not be known to be absolutely immutable; it is only relatively unchanging; in the same way, the light of a *creature* is not infallible by its own efficacy; both have, in fact, proceeded from non-being to being. With this in mind, let us return to our data: for objects, the things of experience; and for the faculty of understanding, a possible and active intellect —these are never more than creatures. It is impossible to give a reason for the certitude which characterizes knowledge without having recourse to the uncreated: "the light that gives infallibility to him who knows and the truth that gives immutability to the thing known." We must have contact with this light and truth which, since it is God himself, cannot be a simple effect of God. Bonaventure develops his thought in subsequent questions: since they are identical with the divine essence, the Ideas which are involved in the knowledge of the Word can regulate our thought without mediation. We encounter again the regulating presence that Grosseteste taught: we see the elaboration, supported by texts from Augustine, of the notion of "Augustinian illumination." Regulating the act of thinking, the *ratio aeterna ut regulans:* God as the Idea acts on the mind without intermediary; He never becomes the object that is seen. The content of our knowledge of things does not come from Ideas, but from things; on this point Aristotle was right in rejecting Plato. Otherwise, human knowledge as such would be confounded with that of the Word, nature with grace, *knowledge* with *wisdom.* Only the sage comes into contact with the eternal and knows it—*scit se illas attingere;* the mere certitude of knowing does not involve this realization of its divine basis, a realization which presupposes a transforming influence of God on man. While wisdom has a mystical character, knowledge is founded on a presence without influence—*praesentia sine influentia.* The illumination that certitude requires is found on the lowest level of the intellectual life. On this same level, the Ideas and the Word, their infinite abode, must be present. This Word is recognized even by faith: *unus est magister vester Christus*—"Christ is your only Master." This is the famous identification of the interior Master with Christ, a being of the flesh, that can be found again in Malebranche.

A formula of this sort leads us to the center of both the thought and the life of St. Bonaventure, a Franciscan from his youth, a general of the Order, the author of a life of the founder. St. Francis had considered himself "a simple and unlearned man" and had cautioned his disciples about the perils of learning. Nevertheless, studies did flourish among the Friars Minor with both rapidity and brilliance. St. Bonaventure was not at all astonished at this; on the contrary, he admired the fact that the Franciscan movement had developed in the image of the Church, beginning with simple preachers but later producing celebrated and learned doctors. He had himself followed the lectures of Alexander of Hales; he entered the Order at a time when learned men had already come to share the life of simple men. A Franciscan then would not be forbidden to study, but the object of his study ought to be Christian wisdom, *sapientia christiana.* St. Francis could repeat the Pauline words: "I have never claimed to know any thing among you, save Jesus Christ, and him crucified." Even when fortified with an encyclopedic knowledge, his disciples had to be able to repeat this in complete sincerity. From this was derived the conception of knowledge proposed by St. Bonaventure: *ipse [Christus] est medium omnium scientiarum*—Christ himself "is the center of all the sciences." This "Christocentrism" held not only for theology but for all knowledge. Let us examine the case of metaphysics.

A great debate, Aristotle's conflict with Platonism, runs through the history of this discipline, for the Philosopher detests the Ideas of Plato—*exsecratur ideas Platonis.* This position of Aristotle explains all the errors Arabic Peripateticism brought to Christianity. A single example will suffice: If there were no Ideas, God would not know other beings; but in fact a providence must embrace a knowledge of all things in particular. In the *Timaeus,* however, there is a notion of providence; in positing his Ideas, Plato at least takes the right road; at the end is St. Augustine, for whom the Word is the abode of the Ideas. When in this way one admits the existence of an "eternal art," of some "exemplars," in the divinity, the great metaphysical problems are clarified and can be reduced to two: How do beings come out from their source, and how do they return to it? Philosophers cannot comprehend a multitude of beings proceeding from a principle which remains immutable. "They deny that arising from one and the same being, which always remains the same, diverse beings exist"—*Negant quod ab uno et eodem, semper manente eodem, sint multiformia.* For Avicenna, only *one* Intelligence can proceed from his First Being. The biblical creation, on the contrary, consists in the direct dependence of a diversity of beings on the divine unity. One acquires this point of view by believing in Christ. "The entrance into these things," says Bonaventure, "consists in understanding the incarnate Word which is the root of the comprehension of all things; moreover, he who does not have access to this entrance cannot penetrate. And the philosophers hold as impossible that which is supremely true, because the entrance is closed for them" —*Horum ostium est intellectus Verbi incarnati qui est radix intelligentiae omnium, unde qui non habet hoc ostium, intrare non potest. Philosophi autem habent pro impossibili quae sunt summe vera, quia ostium est eis clausum.* When confronted with the philosophers, who deny the creation, St. Bonaventure takes up the *nisi credideritis, non intelligetis*—not believing in the Incarnation, infidels do not know the Word, through whom heaven and earth have been created. The believer, however, can refer to relationships existing between the Persons of the Trinity. The Father, in the Son whom He begets, expresses not only what He is, but all that He can do, and by encompassing all that is possible, the future as well. As the likeness of God, the Word is also the exemplar of all things. His generation coincides with the conception of the Ideas, as numerous as the multitude of possibilities. The Son is the "Art" of the Father and the means of making the multiplicity of beings emanate from the divinity; moreover, the Son is seen as the very truth upon which all certain knowledge is based. In our sketch of the theory of illumination, we have seen in it the lowest level of the spiritual life, the first step in the return of creatures to the Creator. Whether one discusses creation or illumination, the Word constitutes the central figure: God acting as a universal exemplar—*in ratione omnia exemplantis*—such is the metaphysician's point of view, grasping here a principle of knowledge which is identical with being—*idem est principium essendi et cognoscendi.*

This principle is revealed to us in Christ; in following St. Bonaventure, we have, by means of the Word, thought of the Ideas as a function of the Trinity. Is this not a mingling of philosophy with theology? It may be. But if there is a mingling, the Franciscan doctor has done it consciously. He was not unaware that philosophy aspires to be a science, the work of reason, and that theology begins with faith, founded on authority. He taught that there is the same difference between knowing and believing as between grasping an object by the intellect and apprehending it by love. But when the object is God, one can both know and believe the same things about Him. However compelling the results of its operation may be, our reason never procures for us the vision of the divine essence, an intuition whose evidence would banish faith, but whose absence hollows out in the mind the place for faith. When a man has proven the unity of God, he does not yet see how the divine manner of being *one* is compatible with the fact of being *three;* under pain of error this must be believed.

We come to a crucial point when the theologian encounters the God of the Peripatetic philosophers. "Let us suppose," he says, "that a man possesses natural and metaphysical knowledge extending to surpreme substances and that after arriving he remains there; he cannot do this without falling into error, unless he is aided by the light of faith, which teaches that God is both three and one, supremely powerful and a supremely efficacious goodness." St. Bonaventure does not find these characteristics of the true God in the First Being of Arabic Aristotelianism: a trinity of persons; a power and a goodness which, laughing at the hierarchy of causes and the succession of Intelligences, constitutes the immediate, radical principle of all reality. "If you think otherwise," the theologian says to the philosopher, "you are, with respect to divine things, a fool"—*Si aliter credas, insanis supra Deum.* Here the cortege of Peripatetics follows in the train of St. Anselm's *insipiens.* There is only one God, the one of faith, to whom, in man, *one* thought must correspond. Too much must not be believed too quickly: to stop with the attributes which it suffices reason to know, as if this were all, would be to disregard what divinity possesses beyond these attributes in the unity of a single essence. From this point of view, philosophical speculation arrives at truth only for those minds that are aware of what surpasses reason—that is, the Revelation with which the theologian begins.

Let us not force Bonaventure to cease thinking about what he believes when he engages in metaphysics: this would be to ask him to deliberately place himself outside the conditions he himself established in this regard for true thought. He will philosophize in the direction of a theology. "Philosophical knowledge is a road toward other knowledge; he who would stop there falls into darkness." Such was the fate of the philosophers, who saw an end in metaphysics: their wisdom has turned into folly. "He who trusts in philosophical knowledge has become a fool when, for example, he believes that it is possible with this knowledge, but without ulterior light, to apprehend the Creator" —*Qui confidit in scientia philosophica . . . , stultus factus est, scilicet quando per istam scientiam sine ulteriori lumine credit se apprehendere Creatorem.* On this point the arrival in the West of Aristotle and the Arabs leaves the tradition of St. Anselm intact. The conflict between philosophical theses and the articles of faith serves to confirm the latter; the errors of the philosophers demonstrate the destiny awaiting those who would attempt to understand without believing: the same men who knew many true things about God were mistaken about many others. This indicates that knowledge makes faith absolutely necessary rather than superfluous.

From knowledge of the Creator, the influence of faith

descends into Bonaventure's conception of the world. To know the creature is, in effect, to see it *created,* to grasp it in relation to its source. For "it is not possible to arrive at the knowledge of a creature except by passing through that by which it has been made"—*ad notitiam creaturae perveniri non potest nisi per id per quod facta est.* It will then be necessary to refer everything to its Idea, to its model in the Word, to consider it as an image or rather as a "vestige." (If tradition actually reserves the quality of being an "image" of God for rational souls alone, to Bonaventure every creature, even in its essence, seems to be a "vestige"—an imitation far removed—of the Creator.) To be a vestige is not, for any creature, an *accident— esse vestigium nulli accidit creaturae.* It is then a misunderstanding of the essence of beings to treat them as things absolutely established; when thinking about them, they must be related to the transcendent reasons they imitate, and for which they constitute, as it were, the sensible signs. *Creaturae possunt considerari ut res vel ut signa.* Creatures may be dealt with either as *things* or as *signs:* the opposition of these two points of view is apparently fundamental. On the one hand, the world is seen in terms of Aristotelian natural philosophy; on the other, it is seen in terms of a sacred symbolism. And, in the latter case, the position adopted by St. Bonaventure, we discover not only the traditional comparison of the visible world to a book which speaks to us about God in a way that is neither less important nor different than Scripture; we also find the new vision of things recently suggested by Francis of Assisi, in whose mind each of their qualities evoked a divine perfection.

The "natural philosophy" of the first point of view is concerned with analyzing the nature of things but without seeking a higher significance. By deviating from his master, Aristotle followed this path. When Plato posited his Ideas, he pointed out in effect that data derived from sensory perception was not sufficient for thought; a man of the hereafter, he was an "illuminated philosopher"; a divine gift had set him in the right direction. Aristotle, on the other hand, truly exemplifies natural reason—too natural, if one may say so, since human nature has been put off balance by Adam's sin. The revelation of original sin serves to clarify the position of the Philosopher, to further justify recourse to faith. It is enough to briefly describe the disequilibrium that followed the original Fall, and from which new falls proceed. This loss of balance consists in a diminished interest in the intelligible and divine order, in a greater attraction for the sensible order. Loved for themselves, beings do not suggest to the mind anything beyond themselves, they no longer constitute signs, but only things, seen as absolute ends in themselves. When, however, concupiscence is eliminated from the human heart, all beings will immediately remind a purified, detached mind of the God who made them; creatures, if they reach the highest level, will be permitted to see the Creator, as if things themselves were transparent, just as Francis of Assisi saw Him in all things. This saint was a mystic, an *ecstatic:* because love gave him another soul, he saw the world in a way different from the rest of men. With respect to the knowledge of creatures, we return not only to Anselm's problem of understanding, but also to Bernard's problem of love; in St. Bonaventure's *Itinerarium mentis in Deum*—the description of a route leading the mind to God—we hear an echo of Anselm and Bernard, as well as of Richard of Saint-Victor: it is the perfect union of scholasticism and mysticism. Let us recall that the divine basis for *knowledge* is apparent only to the conscience of a soul transformed by true *wisdom*—the wisdom Denis extolled, the experience born of a grace. In closing our discussion of Bonaventure, we must deal with it.

In the fifth and sixth chapters of the *Itinerarium*, the intellect considers divine things in themselves. The first consideration is founded on the Being who said: "I am who am." Once again we encounter "the metaphysics of Exodus"; this is the point of view of the Old Testament, of the unity of God. In the following chapter, the discussion turns on the Trinity—that is, on the New Testament; the Good is the point of departure: "No one is good but God alone." In the framework of this double point of departure, both Scripture and tradition in turn propose, as names for God, the "Being" and the "Good." When the attention is focused on the Being, it is possible to see what He is, in himself, with such a degree of certainty that it is impossible to think that He is not—*ipsum esse adeo in se certissimum, quod non potest cogitari non esse.*

At this point, the argument of the *Proslogion* tends toward the simplicity of a proof. But St. Bonaventure reasons about the Being, knowing that it is identical with the Truth which enlightens us; elsewhere he says that "the highest truth is the same being than which nothing greater can be thought." In this way, St. Augustine is linked with St. Anselm. This time we shall find in the texts themselves such classic problems in the history of philosophy as "vision in God," and the "innateness" of the idea of God. But let us merely note that the Franciscan doctor still uses dialectic, and that although he works toward a proof, he does not find it; still less does he find given in an intuition a clear concept of the very essence of God. All that follows makes this intellectual situation apparent. When he has finished considering the attributes of the divine nature by beginning with the Being, his mind adopts the other point of view, that of the Good, to envision the properties of the Persons: we see him turn, as it were, around his object. This new consideration results in a proof of the Trinity based on the principle that "it is said that the good tends to diffuse itself; the Sovereign Good then tends to diffuse itself in the highest degree" —*bonum dicitur diffusivum sui; summum igitur bonum summe diffusivum sui.* When he has shown that the diffusion of the good does not attain to the supreme degree except among the three divine Persons, the theologian has accomplished his task. We do not have time to seek what St. Bonaventure owes here to Richard of Saint-Victor and

to Alexander of Hales; leaving such details aside, let us
keep to the spirit of his argument: to prove that God "is
in such a fashion that it is not possible to think about
Him correctly without thinking Him trine and one"—
*sic est, quod non potest recte cogitari, quin cogitetur
trinum et unum.* Even to our mind the Trinity appears
essential with the same necessity that assures Anselm of
the existence of God. This intelligibility of the divine however does not remove the obscurity of faith, nor transform
it into vision. But by considering the perfections of the
Being, the mind already has in it the wherewithal to be
raised up in admiration—*habes unde subleveris in ad-
mirationem.* When he grasps the necessity of the Trinity
by the communicability of the Good, the theologian does
not think that he comprehends what remains incomprehensible. His admiration believes; the mind is, in the
strongest possible sense of the word, astonished—*in stu-
porem admirationis.* The emotional part of the soul expands: there is no central intuition to unite in a single
thought all these truths which, one after another, have
been proven necessary; only the awareness of a vast,
expanding mystery can be found.

Once again the Incarnation appears as given with the
Trinity. (We are still concerned with the sixth chapter
of the *Itinerarium,* inspired by the New Testament.) The
object to be considered coincides with the object that
eternal life will disclose: "the only true God and Jesus
Christ whom he sent." Meditating on this text, one grasps
the "essential and personal conditions" of the divinity, no
longer considered in themselves, but in their relationship
to the union of God and man in Christ which surpasses
wonder—*supermirabilis.* The Creator and creature exist together, all in one: we are in the midst of a doctrine in
which, after having considered absolute Being, the Good
in itself, and the Trinity as the manifestation of its supreme
fecundity, there is still the Incarnation, situated beyond
and above our line of thought. The soul approaches the
point where, knowledge failing, it proceeds further only

through sentiment—*ibi non intrat intellectus sed affectus.*
This exaltation of love, to be expected in a disciple of the
Poor Man of Assisi, must not obscure either the complexity
or the profoundly intellectual aspect of Bonaventure's conception of ecstasy (*excessus*). It is defined not by the
absence of intuition, but by the infinity of its object. To the
objectum excedens corresponds, in the order of knowledge,
the *modus excessivus;* thus the soul of Christ is in ecstasy in
the very vision of the Word—*contuendo excedit.* As "the
joy of the Lord" exceeds the heart of man, so the infinite
foundation of knowledge surpasses every finite mind. In
order to apprehend it or rather to allow oneself "to be
taken" by it, its infinity requires a leaving of oneself, a
passage into the Other—the frame of mind, in itself
obscure, by which ecstasy is expressed.

The work of St. Bonaventure seems to be an original
synthesis, but what the "philosophers" contributed to it is
less important than what was derived from the earlier
Christian speculative and spiritual tradition. By recognizing
its mystical character, as we have done, it is not reduced
to an emotional level. Its intellectual structure prohibits
considering it, as has been done, as "Augustinian" confusion, when contrasted with Thomistic distinctions. In a
similar vein, some would consider the writings of Albert
the Great,[5] the Dominican master of St. Thomas, merely
as a preparation for Thomism. In the present state of our
knowledge, it is perhaps better not to attempt to decide
the significance of his immense work. Albert seems to have
been an encyclopedist who sought to share his knowledge
of Greeks, Arabs, and Jews with his Latin contemporaries;
he especially wanted to make the books of Aristotle intelligible to them. He had an understanding of his role in

[5] Albert of Bollstädt, born in 1206 in Lavingen (Swabia),
entered the Dominican Order in 1223, and taught at Paris
(1240-48). There Thomas Aquinas was his student (1245-48).
The greater part of his teaching was done in Cologne, where
he died *c.* 1280. He was canonized in 1931, and is now referred to as St. Albertus Magnus or St. Albert the Great.

the *translatio studii,* and he assumed it with a "Renaissance" enthusiasm.

The historian asks what significance Aristotle had for Albert. Albert saw not only the abstract technique and the idea of nature, but also the concrete natures of beings, given solely to experience: he wanted to be an observer. In the speculative order, his Peripateticism is very confused, principally because of the influence of Avicenna and his extensive utilization of Platonism. When he discusses the soul, for example, he agrees with Plato by defining it in itself as a spirit, an incorporeal substance, and with Aristotle by calling it the form of a body—a characteristic that consequently does not constitute its essence. Albert borrowed this principle of conciliation from Avicenna; elsewhere he followed Averroës on the role of the two intellects, now reintegrated in the soul. In addition, throughout his career he utilized the idea of illumination by "the universal active intellect"—the God of Augustine and Denis. It is perhaps a pervading Dionysian inspiration that tends to unify his immense philosophical erudition with a more personal theology. Surviving his student Thomas Aquinas, Albert seems to have been surprisingly faithful to the philosophical positions of his youth. Less organized and philosophically much less original than the work of his great disciple, his thought appears to be more ample, rich in possibilities other than Thomism: these will later be developed by other Dominicans.

The contemporary revival of Thomism has not been, as one would expect, very useful for a real understanding of St. Thomas.[6] We have, to be sure, a precise conception of the totality of his theses. For the Thomists it is a system, independent of its time, a total synthesis of unique perfection. Focusing on its sources, others have seen in the same work merely "a mosaic in which a multitude of

[6] Thomas Aquinas was born in the castle of Roccasecca, near Aquino, in 1225; he studied in Naples and then, under Albert the Great, in Paris and Cologne. He became a master of theology in 1256 and taught at Paris from 1256 to 1259 and from 1268 to 1272; he died in 1274.

borrowed fragments, clearly recognizable and
from one another, are juxtaposed." When confront.._
the structure of the *Summa theologica*—a succession of
questions, divided into articles, each provided with an
apparatus of arguments pro and con—certain of our contemporaries wonder if a Thomistic system really exists
and, if so, what it is. To answer this statement of the problem, let us not set forth the more or less successful adjust-
ment of concepts in the writings of Thomas Aquinas; let
us search rather in the order of intentions, which give
unity to living thoughts, compounded from and based
on received elements—seeing them in a given time and
place. A completed work can be detached from its age,
but then it is no longer possible to understand what the
author sought to accomplish.

We already have some knowledge of the intellectual
atmosphere of the first half of the thirteenth century: the
influence of Avicenna was mingled there with that of
St. Augustine; even when the active intellect was not
"separated," all certain knowledge demanded a divine
illumination. Let us imagine Thomas Aquinas in these surroundings: there his texts take on life. When he comments
on the *Sentences,* he does not distinguish between Avicenna and Aristotle in his theory of the intellect; he
thinks that all the philosophers explain our knowledge by
the action of a separated intelligence. Avicennianism applied its general conception of the production of forms in
the world to the production of intelligibles in us. The
separated intellect is identical with the *dator formarum;*
what it alone gives, the soul and the body merely prepare
to receive. Our activity, like that of things, comes from an
external principle. St. Thomas, on the contrary, favors an
internal principle, a *nature* which by itself accomplishes
its own operation. From this point of view, the active intellect becomes a *part* of the soul, multiplying itself with
individual souls instead of remaining unique in its transcendence, as the Intelligence or God. "For it does not
seem probable that in the rational soul there would not

be a principle by which it could perform its natural operation; this is what follows if only one active intellect is
posited, whether it is called God or Intelligence"—*Non
enim videtur probabile quod in anima rationali non sit
principium aliquod quo naturalem operationem explere
possit: quod sequitur, si ponatur unus intellectus agens,
sive dicatur Deus, vel intelligentia.* Let us reject not only
the unity of the possible intellect in Averroës, but also the
unity of the active intellect in Avicenna and in most of
the philosophers. As many men as there are, so many
principles of this kind exist. This is a requirement that
will not be satisfied by substituting the Word for the Intelligence of the Arabs.

Thomas Aquinas sees that Christians have accom-
modated Avicennianism to the Gospel of St. John: the
Arabic doctrine of the separated Intelligence "cannot be
defended according to faith. And this is why certain
Catholic doctors, correcting this opinion and in part following it, have posited with sufficient probability that
God himself is the active intellect, since by cleaving to
Him our soul finds beatitude; and they confirm this idea
by citing John 1. 9: He was the true Light, which lighteth
every man . . ."—*hoc secundum fidem non potest sustineri. Et ideo quidam catholici doctores, corrigentes hanc
opinionem et partim sequentes, satis probabiliter posuerunt ipsum Deum esse intellectum agentem, quia per ap-
plicationem ad ipsum, anima nostra beata est et hoc
confirmant per hoc quod dicitur, Joh. I, ix: Erat lux vera,
quae illuminat omnem hominem. . . .* Let us note here
the clear perception of the thirteenth-century situation:
from the viewpoint of faith, the Dominican doctor understands and appreciates "Avicennian Augustianism." To
set it aside, he has only a notion of nature, as a constituent of all being. Let us grant the force of this idea: the
illumination dear to Saint Augustine will no longer be
expressed by speaking of God as the active intellect. Instead, the active intellect will be made a part of the
soul so that the soul can truly act; illumination will be the

gift of this natural light, efficacious for the intelligibles which it extracts from the sensible.

The Thomistic path deviates as much from the direction St. Bonaventure followed as from the tradition of Guillaume d'Auvergne and Roger Bacon. In thought we no longer seek an act, such as the *cognitio certitudinalis,* which would include divine assistance under a special title: the operation of a creature on so high a plane that the creature itself would be powerless. From St. Augustine's thought, let us preserve only the idea that God is the source of our intellections—as he is of all things. As Gilson has remarked, "the problem of knowledge is only a particular case of the problem of the efficacy of second causes." On this question, Thomism is in opposition to Eastern Peripateticism. In the *Summa contra Gentiles,* Avicebron (the Jewish philosopher Ibn Gabirol) appears before Avicenna to suggest to us a radical theory of the activity of God and the passivity of things: the divine will, as a spiritual principle, penetrates all bodies subject to it by its unique efficacy, so that they have only the appearance of action. "Avicebron," we are told, "affirms that no body is active, but that the power of the spiritual substance, by penetrating bodies, accomplishes all the actions which seem to be effected by bodies"—*ponit Avicebron quod nullum corpus est activum, sed quod virtus substantiae spiritualis, pertransiens per corpora, agit actiones quae per corpora fieri videntur.* The Jewish thinker intended to exalt the power of God; to increase the efficacy of the First Agent, was, for Avicebron, to celebrate His name—*quanto magis virtus factoris primi, excelsum nomen ejus.*

To understand Thomism as a thirteenth-century metaphysics, one must enter into these authors' physical concepts. Avicenna entangled his theory of knowledge in a cosmogony. Ibn Gabirol held that nothing corporeal constitutes an active cause. As for St. Thomas, his position places us in the midst of Aristotelian natural philosophy, in the very center of this science of *natures.* Bodies are composites of matter and form; all concrete beings, even those that are inanimate, include a principle of activity, comparable to some definite tendency or to life itself— the *nature* of fire makes it warming, that of man makes him engender man. For a moment let us forget the Cartesian revolution, and try to live in a realm of substantial forms. Let us even consider Platonism from an Aristotelian point of view. Then we will think that Plato has unduly separated forms from beings, in order to make them his Ideas; that consequently, in his doctrine, things have become merely passive matter; that the activity they present to the senses must be attributed to some transcendent principle—whether to the Ideas or the Intelligence of God himself, it matters little. In any case, sensible beings are emptied of an essential part of their reality, for the benefit of a *beyond*. St. Thomas makes Plato the predecessor of all thinkers who, surrendering to this tradition, take from natural beings their proper actions—*qui rebus naturalibus proprias subtrahunt actiones.*

By adopting the opposite attitude with Aristotle, our Dominican maintains the reality of *this* world. Thus, in his theory of knowledge, the active intellect, as a *part* of the soul, belongs to the form of a body; Thomistic man is a "natural being" who, even with respect to knowledge, preserves his "own action." In this sense, one can use the term "naturalism" to designate what Thomas Aquinas took from Aristotle rather than from Avicenna. It does not seem to have been his intention in this matter to set aside the dangers that menaced faith: Christians had known how to correct Avicennianism. To explain Thomism, it is then necessary to admit a rational value—either real or apparent—for the idea of nature. The historian, Gilson has said, finds here "a purely philosophical decision." It is true that this central idea, in St. Thomas as in Aristotle, is the one which Descartes will eliminate when founding his physics and ours, the same that Malebranche will denounce for its latent paganism. (Must a monotheist not reserve efficacy for God? We are reminded of the

Jewish philosopher Ibn Gabirol.) We touch here what is perhaps the greatest difficulty encountered today in demonstrating that in Thomism there is a mode of rational thought: when it is presented as a "Christian philosophy," it is necessary to gain acceptance not only for the union of these two words, but also for the application of the first to a work of reason imbued with Aristotelian natural philosophy.

With this example we can indicate the degree to which Descartes separates us from the Middle Ages. But Malebranche leads us, as if by antithesis, to a better understanding of Thomism. In order to give the opposite answer, he asks in effect the important question: How can a world of *natures* be in accord with the biblical God? St. Thomas's point of view was the following: "God by himself can produce all natural effects; that other causes may also produce them is not however superfluous. This does not in fact result from a lack of power, but from an immensity of goodness: as a consequence of goodness, God wished to communicate His resemblance to things, to such a degree that they not only exist, but that they are also in turn causes." This will become a classic view in the universities: the power of God would be sufficient for everything; His goodness explains why He bestowed efficacy on other beings. To deprive creatures of an activity that is *theirs*, is to slight the Creator: *Detrahere actiones proprias rebus est divinae bonitati derogare*— "To take from things their proper actions is derogatory to divine goodness." Let us say then that although committed to Aristotelian naturalism, Thomas Aquinas sees in the idea of God something on which he can base it. We are dealing here with a decisive point in his thought, which Gilson characterizes in these terms: "A world of efficacious second causes, such as Aristotle's, is worthy only of a God whose causality consists essentially in goodness." The thirteenth-century Dominican doubtlessly found this act of generosity that assimilates creatures to the Creator in the writings of the Pseudo-Denis, which taught

that of all things, the most divine is to become the co-
operator of God—*omnium divinius est Dei cooperatorem
fieri.*

If today we find it difficult to comprehend the kind of
evidence that was able to present the substantial forms
as a system of natural philosophy, we can more easily
grasp the bond that a religious mind was able to find between a creating Goodness and acting creatures. This
perspective on Thomism has the advantage of elucidating
the rest of the Middle Ages. And among the second
causes which contribute efficaciously to the divine work,
we must number ourselves, since the Apostle calls us the
co-operators of God—*Dei sumus adjutores.* Such is the
dignity of human nature. In this naturalism there is also
a humanism, since man is a "nature in Nature," even
though he knows, and his action is regulated by a "cosmic
morality." The knowing being is not a mere subject,
opposed to the world, but in the world, the human composite whose soul is defined as the form of the body: "It
is not either the senses or the intellect which knows, but
man who knows through the action of both." The nature
of the human intellect performs its function: to make an
abstraction from the structure of the sensible, in itself
determined by the theory of individuation and the concept of matter. As for Thomistic ethics, it may be said that
they are oriented "strictly toward the point of view of the
metaphysical finality of Aristotelian nature" (Rohmer),
provided "metaphysical" is underlined and refers to the
Being who created through goodness. In this context, the
man who understands the significance of his human grandeur will be able to "judge himself worthy of great things"
(Gauthier)—*se magnis dignificat*—in consideration of the
gifts he has received from God.

To understand Thomistic naturalism, we must introduce
an idea of God. Is this not to abandon pure philosophy for
theology? It does not seem so, for alongside theology as a
part of sacred doctrine—*theologia quae ad sacram doc-
trinam pertinet*—the *Summa theologica* recognizes an-

other sort that constitutes a part of philosophy—*quae pars philosophiae ponitur*. Let us say that a "natural theology" and a "revealed theology" are distinguished as being essentially different (*secundum genus*). The foundations of the way to knowledge are so diverse here that the two disciplines can treat the same object without useless repetition. Some truths accessible to reason are in fact found to have been revealed—for example, the very idea of God that we have just discussed. How can this be explained? When, by definition, natural light suffices in the whole realm of philosophy, for what purpose do we receive a revelation about the same matters? The *Summa theologica* teaches: "Even concerning those things about God that can be discerned by human reason, it was necessary that man be instructed by divine Revelation; for, when sought by reason, truth relative to God would come to man only in a *small number of minds, after a long delay, mingled with numerous errors;* on this truth however, depends the salvation of man, which is in God." *A paucis, et per longum tempus, et cum admixtione multorum errorum*—thus speaks the experience of philosophy, when examined by the theologian. As a consequence, not only was it practically necessary for God to reveal truths knowable through natural light, but these truths must also be considered as knowable by divine light: *divino lumine cognoscibilia*—or, in a word, as *revelabilia*, "revealable." When applied to truths rationally accessible to natural theology, this term indicates that they belong to the realms of both faith and reason. Our problem consists in maintaining an essential distinction and at the same time grasping a fundamental point: in Gilson's *Christian Philosophy of St. Thomas Aquinas*, this concept of the "revealable" makes it possible to comprehend how St. Thomas "integrated" his philosophy into theology without corrupting either "the purity of revelation" or of reason.

Thomistic theology is "the science of revelation." The Parisian Dominican, Guillaume d'Auxerre, had already written: "If theology did not admit of principles, it would not be an art or a science. It does then have principles, namely the articles of faith, which however constitute principles only for believers; and for them they are things known in themselves that have no need of external proof." By taking up this concept, and comparing the articles of faith to principles, Thomistic theology disclaims all attempts to give proofs for them: "It does not have the means to prove them, since no art can prove its principles, but only to defend them against those who deny them." By definition, the principles are undemonstrable, even for the science that they found. A superior discipline could prove them—if it were to exist; when Aristotle came to primary philosophy, and encountered individuals who rejected its principles, he could only refute their arguments. Let us transpose this: the theologian, who must answer the objections of the unbeliever, would not know how to prove the articles of faith according to the concept of demonstration belonging to the idea of science. This incapacity can be illustrated in the case of the Trinity. Thomas Aquinas knows of three ways to prove the plurality of the divine Persons: by the infinity of Goodness diffusing itself (we are reminded of St. Bonaventure), by the tendency to share the enjoyment of a good (this is reminiscent of Richard of Saint-Victor), and by the word and the love of our soul, as a divine image (this is the method of the *Monologion*). Our doctor rejects the first two; as for the third, which he follows, he does not consider it an adequate proof of what takes place in God, but simply as a way of describing it. He indicates his position by saying that through natural reason it is impossible to attain knowledge of the Trinity. In effect, an intellect that begins with the sensible infers the Creator from creatures; but—and this is a classical thesis in theology—the creative action is common to all three Persons; when one comes to God as the Creator, only the unity of His essence can be found. For St. Thomas, the possibility of proving a truth seems to have been confounded with the possibility of acquiring it. Conversely, with respect to the same problem,

Anselm, Richard, and St. Bonaventure seem to have assumed, as Gilson has said, that "human reason was capable of proving knowledge that it was incapable of acquiring." The *necessity* of those reasons that led to "the understanding of faith" were due to the fact that the understanding asserted the impossibility of rejecting truth received through Revelation. In Thomism the domain of proof, in the sense of demonstration, appears to be limited by the *natural* light of man, which itself is defined with reference to the sensible.

To defend a dogma, the theologian can demonstrate the inanity of the objections raised against it; in the case of a dogma accepted as a premise, he can also proceed with the rigorous deduction of conclusions. But when applied to the articles of faith itself, to truths that are only revealed, theological reasoning can only serve to expound (*declarare*), to illustrate (*manifestare*) those truths that have already been posited, without ever constraining the mind to admit them; never demonstrative, merely "probable," more or less "persuasive," becoming a mockery if it attempts demonstration, it finds its place in the realm of the comparisons or images (*similitudines*) of which Augustine's *De trinitate* made abundant use. By what right can these indemonstrable concepts, completely lacking any proof, be the principles of a "science"? By the divine right of faith, which, being a transcendent gift and not something acquired by human means, lifts our mind above itself, imprinting on it something of divine knowledge—*impressio divinae scientiae*. It has been said of the theologian adhering to revelation by this "infused light" that "Faith is his nearest principle, but his first principle is the divine intellect in which he believes." Now, in the divine intellect, and in the intellects of the blessed who see God, these truths, which for us are of faith, are self-evident. Let us not isolate on high the theology of men here below; let us consider its relationship, its "subalternation," to the intuitive knowledge of God and the blessed—*scientia Dei et beatorum*—in which the principles that theology *believes* are *seen*. The theologian's work appears as "science" to the degree that, through the twofold grace of Revelation and faith, it thus finds itself in contact with a divine understanding which is, in a precise sense, knowledge in itself (Duméry).

The same communication with divine knowledge, in the transcendence of faith, permits theology to develop in an order that is proper to it. Having received the truths that he cannot acquire, the believer no longer follows the philosophical order, which begins with the sensible. Instead, he orders his entire intellectual life as a function of these transcendent data, and lifts himself up toward God. At the same time that it is a definition of nature, Thomism admits of a reversal of its perspective: its most exact interpreter—whom we have had to cite so often—has written that Aquinas "established reason in the realm of the sensible as its proper domain, but, by equipping it for the exploration and conquest of this domain, he invites it to turn its glances by preference toward another sphere which is no longer merely the domain of man, but that of the children of God." As a human creation, pure philosophy ought to conform to the definition of man: an intellect naturally united to a body which apprehends the intelligible by beginning with the sensible; the order of his knowledge moves from things to God.

The *Summa theologica* and even the *Summa contra Gentiles* follow the reverse order: from the Creator to creatures. This is the order of *doctrina sacra*, which, having received the truth about God through Revelation, expounds this data in imitation of divine knowledge: the divinity knows itself and consequently knows that all things are relative to it. Let us be careful not to apply to the *Summae* the modern idea of an autonomous system of pure reason, where each truth is presented in its place, in an order of invention. This is rather a system of faith, an order of exposition, which in certain instances admits purely rational truths according to their utility. Gilson has stated the Thomistic point of view on rationality as follows: "When St. Thomas speaks as a philosopher, he deals only with his demonstrations that are on trial, and it matters little that the thesis he sustains may appear in terms that faith assigns to it, since he never cites the authority of faith, and never asks us to do so in a proof that he considers rationally demonstrable." The historian then can find philosophical questions, but they are treated in a theological order. If, with Gilson, he presents them in this order, he will expound "the philosophy of St. Thomas" in the only way that the great Dominican "expounded it himself." Let us be precise about what he had to expound since, accepting "a transcending influence of faith over reason," he saw even rational truths in a different light, that is, as "revealable"—"revealability" implying "the permanent disposition of all knowledge in view of the theologian's work."

Within this order, one begins with God, and in the matter of philosophical problems, with the problem of his existence. The properly Thomistic dimension of the latter is derived from St. Thomas's interpretation of the divine statement: "I am who am." "The metaphysics of Exodus" is concerned with "the revealable that has been revealed." In its Thomistic formulation, it expresses the transcendence of God as being, not by saying with Avicenna and Guillaume d'Auvergne that He has no essence, but rather by asserting that His essence consists in *being* itself— *essentia est ipsum suum esse*. It is a question (the use of the verb indicates this) of a single act, of the pure *act* of being, without addition or change—*esse tantum, purum esse*. God, Gilson writes, does not put himself in the realm of essence—"the infinite essence to whom the full right of existence should belong"—but in the order of existence—"the absolute act of existing, in which existence as it were takes the place of essence."

The distinction between these two orders is in fact imposed upon every finite being. Beyond the form (whether this constitutes only an incorporeal substance or whether it is united with matter in a composite), the

Thomistic analysis discerns an act which in itself is being
—*ipsum esse in actu*—the "ultimate" act in finite substance, with respect to which even the form remains
potential. This relationship of potency to act, expresses
the difference between, or to use the classical terminology,
the "real composition" of, finite essence and existence, by
prohibiting the realization of the one without the other,
as two separate *things*—an inherent temptation in the
expression "real distinction." The successors of St.
Thomas, like the Augustinian Giles of Rome, succumbed
to this temptation. Gilson tries to avoid it by holding to
the delicate balance of the interpretation we have just
sketched in a summary fashion. He does not conceal the
difficulty of grasping such a position, incomprehensible to
anyone who identifies "the real with the thinkable and
the thinkable with that which is the object of a concept."
Not only does the Supreme *Being* that is God place
itself "strictly beyond all possible representation," but,
transcending essence, all *esse* "transcends the concept as
well." Provided it is granted that in its pure state, in its
ultimate degree, to exist implies neither becoming nor
restlessness—*aliquid fixum et quietum*—Thomism interpreted in this way may be called a philosophy "of existence" and as a consequence, "of judgment." Correspond-
ing in the mind to existence, as a nonconceptual act, is
the act of judgment, the truth of which, writes Gilson,
"is founded less on the essence of things than on their
esse." Beyond the whole order of essences, it seems that
the dynamism of judgment "alone is capable of attaining"
the divine *esse,* the source of the "dynamism of existence."
Here, Gilson's *Christian Philosophy of St. Thomas
Aquinas* nearly approaches the profound reflections of
Joseph Maréchal in *Le Thomisme devant la philosophie
critique*. In any event, the Thomistic proofs for the existence of God are interpreted as representing the discovery
of a new dimension of being. The universe they disclose
is not that of Aristotle as restored by Averroës: for every
datum, the necessary difference—*oportet quod esse suum*

sit aliud quod ipsum—between the act of being and the thing itself is seen as a consequence of Creation. Without losing the substantiality of "being made to endure," the Aristotelian *natures*—one of which is man in his unity— rest on a "finite act of existence" which refers back to the infinite Act: the Creator. Some twentieth-century theologians would remind modern man, as a historical being, that the biblical God is the Lord of history; by taking over the naturalism of the thirteenth century in a transmutation of Aristotle's metaphysics, the natural theology of St. Thomas established the God of Exodus as the Lord of *natures*. This single development, in Gilson's opinion, carried "Western thought as far beyond the metaphysics of Aristotle as, four centuries later, Descartes would carry it beyond the qualitative physics of the Schoolmen." When interpreted in this way, it can be seen that the fortunes of Thomism appear to be quite independent of the destiny of Aristotelian physics.

St. Thomas immediately became the leader of a school, in spite of the number and the authority of his adversaries in the Church. Some twenty of the propositions condemned in Paris on March 7, 1277, struck at his teaching. Later in the same month, the Dominican archbishop of Canterbury, Robert Kilwardby, proscribed for the University of Oxford thirty propositions which were for the most part Thomistic. His Franciscan successor, John Peckham, who united traditionalism in theology with scientific curiosity, renewed this condemnation in 1284. In January of 1285, he wrote to Rome denouncing Thomism: "May the Holy Roman Church deign to consider that the teaching of the two Orders is actually in almost complete opposition on all questions that may be disputed; the teaching of one of the Orders abandoning and, to a certain extent, scorning the opinions of the Fathers, is founded almost exclusively on the positions of the philosophers, in such a way that the house of the Lord is filled with idols."

Let us note that, even for contemporaries, Thomism possessed a characteristically philosophical aspect. It also had some of the appearances of a renaissance. In June of the same year, John Peckham wrote to the bishop of Lincoln: "You know that we do not in any way disapprove of philosophical studies, in as much as they serve the theological mysteries; but we do disapprove of these profane novelties which, against philosophical truth and to the detriment of the Fathers, were introduced into the depths of theology about twenty years ago, with a manifest rejection and scorn for the theses of the Fathers." The letter then opposes the doctrine "of the sons of St. Francis, Friar Alexander of Hales, and Friar Bonaventure" to "the new doctrine which is almost completely contrary to it." Does this not constitute an attack on "the teaching of St. Augustine on the eternal rules and the immutable light"?

We would like to indicate the destiny of "Augustinian illumination" among the Franciscans after St. Thomas. In the inevitable and always arbitrary choice of authors, we have omitted both Richard of Mediavilla, and the "spiritual" Peter Olivi. By devoting our attention to the Franciscan "school" (it would be better to say "milieu," considering the doctrinal diversity), we leave aside secular masters like Henry of Ghent[7] who adjusted a theory of illumination to a doctrine of natural knowledge in which the "first object" of the human understanding is none other than God, grasped under the generality of "analogical" concepts such as "the being," "the true," or "the good." In the first years of the fourteenth century, Duns Scotus will elaborate his theory of knowledge and many other aspects of his thought by his opposition to Henry of Ghent, whose influence extends beyond his century, at

[7] Richard of Mediavilla taught at Paris from 1283 to 1287. Peter John Olivi (Olieu), born in Sérignan (France) about 1248, died at Narbonne in 1298. Henry of Ghent taught at Paris from 1276 to 1292. Another secular master, Godfrey of Fountaines (active between 1285 and 1304), must at least be mentioned.

least through the criticism some of his theses provoked.

In the Franciscan theory of knowledge there was not a continuous development of Aristotelianism. After having studied it from Alexander of Hales to John Peckham (who lived until 1292), one scholar could write: "Augustinian illumination, turned from its course for an instant, finally recovered all its rights." We have seen that Alexander of Hales and John of La Rochelle had made the active intellect a part of the soul; while admitting this natural light, St. Bonaventure showed its insufficiency to guarantee our knowledge, to establish its certitude. The growth of Aristotelianism and the presence of Thomism seem to have given the Franciscans a lively feeling for the originality of the Augustinianism they espoused. For Aristotle, our senses constitute something passive; man begins to know by receiving the impression of things; to the extent in which it senses, the soul comes into the same plane as bodies, through which it suffers. In this way, Thomas Aquinas thrust us into the world. A scandal from the Augustinian point of view! In such a case, where a body would act on the incorporeal, what becomes of the excellence of the soul? The superior does not suffer from the inferior. A disciple of St. Bonaventure, Matthew of Aquasparta, stresses this difficulty, which he calls on St. Augustine to solve: sensation does not consist in a passion of the soul, issuing from the body, but in an action of this soul on itself, when its body finds itself modified. The details of the doctrine matter little to us. Let us remember that for Augustine, and seemingly for Avicenna, the faculties of sense perception are active and not merely passive. Provided with activity from the sensible in this way, the mind will act again to arrive at the intelligible, but without succeeding by its own light; hence the necessity for divine illumination, an action of the Creator on creatures that must be assigned its place among other influences.

This is not merely the "general influence" of the first cause on all second causes through which the capacity to act is received: this *influentia generalis* is not sufficient, since—St. Bonaventure has taught us—the *cognitio certitudinalis* surpasses all created forces. There can be no question, on the other hand, of a "special influence" (*influentia specialis*), such as grace dispensed for salvation. From a Thomistic point of view, in which it would be necessary to choose either one or the other, our Franciscan would find himself confounded. But he formulates, with great clarity, the Bonaventurian point of view: *in omni opere naturae rationalis, ut rationalis est, cooperatur Deus quodam specialiori modo et quodam specialiori influentia quam in operibus aliorum creaturarum*—With all actions of the rational nature acting as such, God cooperates in a more special fashion, by an influence more special than in the actions of other creatures. Here we have the center for a perspective: when St. Thomas compares knowledge to the operations of a *nature,* the Augustinians[8] emphasize the originality of the intellectual operation of judgment. They are more attached to this concept than to the idea of abstraction, but in both they find the same problem: How is it possible to pass from the datum of sense perception to an intelligible, when the conditions of time and place—that is, mutability—are dropped? The act of the rational creature, the *image* of God, is distinguished from the acts of all other creatures that are mere *vestiges.* Its nature consists in being the image, since grace belongs to a different order, that of *likeness* to God. Nothing is more normal, in this hierarchy of *three* degrees, than being present and acting differently in the likeness than in the image, God should work differently in the image—through illumination—than in the mere vestige. To wish to admit only *two* orders: that of grace and that of all natures, to mock this "influence

[8] A few dates of importance: Matthew of Aquasparta was studying at Paris about 1268; he became a master in theology in 1275, the minister general of the Order in 1287-1289, and died in 1302. Roger Marston died in 1303. Vital du Four taught at Paris, Montpellier, and Toulouse between 1292 and 1300, and died in 1327.

more special than the general without being special," is to deprive oneself of the possibility of understanding the Augustinian interpretation of the specificity of the soul.

If a created understanding can attain certitude—*cognitio certitudinalis*—only by a transcending action, would ignorance of this divine cause not condemn reason to skepticism? A text of Matthew of Aquasparta suggests this problem: as a foundation for knowledge, the principles of natural philosophy are not sufficient, recourse must be made to theological principles—*deficiunt principia philosophiae* (or *physicae*) *et recurrendum ad principia theologiae.* However, the problem posed in this context is not to avoid a philosophically inevitable skepticism by recourse to faith, but to discern the basis for unquestionable certitudes; founded for Averroism in the permanence of the human species, the eternal truth "man is an animal," cannot for the theologian be based on anything created. "Science," concerned with the necessary, seeks the essence (*quidditas*), an abstraction made from experience—an essence that is not reduced to the mere object of a possible human apprehension (*aliquid tantum apprehensibile*), but resting, in illumination, on an Idea, identical with the Eternal. Theology does not intervene to remove a doubt; it permits the description of a fact—the objectivity of knowledge—by recognizing in it a transcendent dimension. The nontemporal force of this Augustinianism can readily be seen.

Foreshadowing Malebranche, John Peckham says that if two of us can conceive of the same truth, this is because we share in the unity of the intellectual light. In this light, Augustine recognized the true God; we can also see in it the active intellect, which Aristotle says is separated, unmoved, constantly in action: these characteristics, however, are proper to God alone. Again we encounter a formula of Avicennian Augustinianism. The same thing is found in Roger Marston, from whom it will be taken up by another Franciscan, Vital du Four. And so we come to the end of the thirteenth century. By saying that only God as the active intellect can complete the illumination of the possible intellect, one finds oneself —as Marston explains well—in agreement with St. Augustine and Catholic truth; for support, it had the text of the Philosopher and the interpretation of his greatest disciples, Al-Farabi and Avicenna. It was not necessary to maintain imprudently that Aristotle did not conceive of the active intellect as a separated substance —a warning to Thomas Aquinas, whom Marston attacks in a lively fashion. We even have a genetic definition of this theory of knowledge, which defends itself so well against Thomism: *sententia sancti Augustini de luce communi omnium, et Philosophi de intellectu agente, sic in concordiam redacta*—"The thought of St. Augustine on the light common to all minds and that of the Philosopher on the active intellect, are thus put into accord." The authorities are shown to be in agreement; one begins with authors. Attempts of this sort are not always without fruit, nor without weakness.

At the end of the century, Peter of Trabes, a contemporary of Peter Olivi, sees the deception of Avicennian Augustinianism: "The thesis that makes of the eternal light the active intellect scorns the words and the thought of Augustine. Indeed it does not seem that he ever divided the intellect into possible and active, or discussed the eternal light of the active intellect, although according to him, this light illuminates our soul. As for his thought, he never either believed or wished that the intellect be possible of that which makes the philosophers posit an active intellect; on the contrary, he everywhere indicates that the intellect is active even though it is illuminated by divine light." The philosophers want an active intellect because, according to their definition, the possible intellect is passivity, receptivity. But the doctrine of St. Augustine excludes all passive possibility from a soul which is superior to the body and has nothing to receive from it; we have already seen Matthew of Aquasparta apply this thesis to sensation. For Peter of Trabes, the intellect is purely active; since it does not act constantly, one may speak of its possibility, but in an active sense. The need for another intellect called active and the distinction of two intellects would appear to be without foundation: the Fathers have never used this division; those who follow the Philosopher, at least in their words, are all in mutual disagreement (*omnes inter se sunt discordes*). When the history of the theories of the intellect in the thirteenth century is examined, one can readily understand Peter's feeling of complication and weariness. Peter of Trabes also says: *nec sancti inveniuntur unquam* (sic) *locuti fuisse*—"The Fathers are not found to have ever spoken in these terms." The tradition of Augustine and Anselm represents here the transcendence of the soul, the activity of the mind. The idea of illumination is transformed: our Franciscan confesses that he does not understand vision in the eternal reasons: *difficile est valde ad intelligendum* ("It is a very difficult thing to grasp)." To see something in God, would this not be merely—if one remains in the natural order—to seize the faculty of knowing from His action? *Dicitur bene: videre in ipso, quia ipse efficit ipsum intellectum, dans ei esse et virtutem ad intelligendum. Et iste est modus communis naturalis cognitionis*—"It is well said: to see in Him, since it is He who causes the intellect by giving it existence and the power to know. Such is the common mode of natural knowledge." This is a fine example of the complexity of historical problems: if Augustinianism is defined by a particular assistance that God could lend to rational operations, this is a negation of it. Like Thomas Aquinas, Peter of Trabes reduces illumination to the gift of an intellect. A victory then for Thomistic naturalism? Perhaps, but only partially. For this does not concern either the intellect or man of Aristotle, entangled by their passivity in the corporeal world. Peter of Trabes is speaking of an intellect and of a soul, derived from Augustine, active and transcendent by essence.

It is from such a point of view that, to join the fourteenth century to the thirteenth, it would be necessary to envisage the teaching of Duns Scotus: subtle, complex, utilizing the two intellects in order to recover the image of God through their complicated mechanism. Let us try to understand the spirit in which it was conceived. Our Franciscan does not want to deprecate the nature of the soul—*vilificare naturam animae*. When he writes, citing Aristotle, that nothing need be posited about any nature which slights its dignity—*in nulla natura ponendum est quod derogat ejus dignitati*—one thinks of the naturalism of St. Thomas. All the more so since Scotus does not admit any particular divine assistance for the acts of knowledge, so that he too seems to reduce illumination to the gift of an intellect. This would seem to represent, in the eyes of an adversary, another victory for Thomism. However, one question may be asked: Are the doctors of the two Orders speaking of the same natural light?

In medieval metaphysics, the nature of a power is defined by its object—the human intellect, in Thomism, by the essence of the sensible thing (*quidditas rei sensibilis*) from which all our concepts are extracted. In the eyes of Duns Scotus, the Thomistic thesis represents the thought of the Philosopher, but a theologian ought not to defend it—*hoc non potest sustineri a theologo*. Holding that *being*, whether it be sensible or not, is the natural object of the intellect, Duns Scotus the theologian—who is influenced himself by Avicenna—by his very definition orients our faculty of knowing toward those intelligible realities from which the sons of Adam have been separated by sin. The Franciscan doctor sees and rejects the reversal of this perspective by which, forsaking the sensible accorded to his reason, the Thomistic man turns by means of faith toward the pure intelligible and the divine. If Thomas Aquinas must have recourse in this way to what has been called a metaphysical "coup d'état," the reason, in the eyes of Duns Scotus, is his inordinate desire to follow the Philosopher, who, as we shall see, not only erred about God but also about man. When

Scotus exalts our intellectual nature (*dignificare naturam*), he is concerned with the soul as conceived by Revelation, beyond what philosophical reason has been able validly to know about it. Here man owes to Revelation the discovery of a *natural* capacity, an enhancement of his *dignity*. When confronted with Aristotelianism, Scotus the theologian does not think that philosophy accords *too much* to man; he feels that it has not given him *enough*. He does not however restrict himself to an exaltation of the natural light of the intellect; he saves something of illumination. Duns Scotus subtly explains the Augustinian expression *intelligere in regulis aeternis* by excluding all "special" intervention: in the perspective of the general influence of God co-operating with man's knowledge as with every natural action, the human understanding knows the necessary truths in "the eternal rules"—the divine ideas. For Scotus these are not strictly co-eternal with the divine essence, the first object of the infinite intellect, the original light; they are the second objects it produces, naturally and necessarily, in their "intelligible being"—still the eternal light, but in a derivative form. When, by means of divine concurrence, a datum derived from experience makes a necessary truth known to a finite understanding, this is due to the essence enclosed in it, to the necessity introduced by the infinite understanding, the source of the possible, in the contingent action of the creating will. Illumination is not reduced to a gift of the intellect, in the creation of the mind; it is the gift to objects of their necessary structure by the divine understanding. Synonomous with the infinite essence, the infinite understanding is not only above beings, it is also above their productions, the finite intelligibles. If it is true that the doctrine of Ideas deserves consideration in the philosophy of religion or in theological criticism (Duméry), the originality of this Scotist position should be remembered.

We have some idea of the development of Franciscan thought between St. Bonaventure and Duns Scotus. Leav-

ing to one side Giles of Rome, the doctor of the Augustinian Hermits, an Order whose intellectual role was not
negligible, let us return to the Dominicans. Those whom
history has preserved as the first Thomists did not all
follow their master in his distinction between essence
and existence; some preferred to remain with Aristotle on
this point. There developed, as Gilson observes, a "Thomism minus the act of being." Of the Dominicans who
were not Thomists, Durand of Saint-Pourçain is the best
known.[9] Durand has often been called a precursor of
William of Ockham, but he is in opposition to Ockham
on a basic issue. In his eyes, relationship constitutes a
mode of being (*esse ad aliud*), which cannot be reduced
to the *esse in se* of a substance, nor to the *esse in alio*
of a quality. This conception enables Durand to teach
a theory of knowledge in which the senses and the intellect are essentially active rather than passive. The fact
of sensation or of knowing has nothing about it of an
absolute reality, which would be added to the soul for
its perfection; it is a mere relationship to the object. The
perfection of the soul is, in fact, such that there is nothing
for it to receive from the outside; by a pure spontaneity
it is related to every object which is presented to it. The
influence of Franciscans such as Peter of Trabes can be
found again here, and St. Augustine is also cited; it is not
surprising then that Durand denies the possible and the
active intellect, as well as the "species"—those forms
which, in Thomism, come to actualize our faculties of
knowing. All of these negations can be understood in
terms of a reaction against the receptivity of the Aristotelian soul.

[9] Durand, born in Saint-Pourçain-sur-Sioule (Allier), was abused
by his Order for his opposition to Thomism; he died as the
bishop of Meaux in 1334. The dates of the three editions of his
Commentary: 1307-8, 1312-13, 1317-27. James of Metz was
another Dominican who was not a Thomist; he taught between
1295 and 1302. Giles of Rome was born about 1247, became a
bachelor in theology in 1276, and died in 1316.

The Dominican Order presents us with still another group of thinkers who form a link in the chain of continuity between Albert the Great and Meister Eckhart. The work of the master of St. Thomas, as we have said, was richer than that of his disciple; the Neoplatonic current passing through it is continued in Ulrich of Strasbourg and Dietrich of Freiberg.[10] The first seems to have been influenced primarily by the *De causis;* the second utilized principally the *Elementatio theologica* of Proclus, which had been translated by William of Moerbeke.

Dietrich was not only a theologian; learned in optics, he has left a remarkable work on the rainbow. To place him in the history of philosophy, let us briefly treat his doctrine of the active intellect. This will be the last example, but not the least, of the speculations and interests covered by this expression in the thirteenth century. Let us at once indicate the double motion of the Neoplatonic world, the *processio* and the *conversio:* "intellectually" all things proceed from the first principle in order to return there. The active intellect emanates from God as his image: all other beings have a divine idea for an exemplar; the active intellect is of the same essence. Things merely imitate an idea, the exemplary form of a determined kind of being—*forma exemplaris alicujus determinati generis entium.* Conforming to the divine essence which does not know this limitation, the intellect has a total, universal character. Let us gather together the more remarkable of Dietrich's statements: The active intellect emanates as an image—in complete conformity with the intellect from which it proceeds and in complete conformity with the divine substance; it proceeds, in fact,

---

[10] Ulrich of Strasbourg, a contemporary of St. Thomas, probably died in 1278. Dietrich of Freiberg died shortly after 1310; he studied and taught at Paris in the last quarter of the century. The exposition of Proclus's *Elements of Theology* by Berthold of Mosburg, another Dominican, will be cited by Nicholas of Cusa.

from the divine *reason* (in the objective sense of essence) in as much as it is the reason for the totality of beings— *Intellectus agens procedit ut imago—in omnimoda conformitate ad intellectum a quo procedit—in omnimoda conformitate ad substantiam divinam—procedit enim a ratione divina prout est ratio universitatis entium.* The divinity not only contains reasons for each being, but it constitutes the reason for all: it is from this that the active intellect proceeds, the perfect image of God and the likeness of all being—*imago Dei perfecta, similitudo totius entis.* If we comprehend the notion of an intellect activated by its essence (*intellectus in actu per suam essentiam*), we will immediately see that the same act by which it emanates from its principle causes it to return to its principle. This act, in fact, can only be an act of intelligence, having this principle for its object. It is this character which defines the image: to proceed as an image is to proceed in knowing that from which one proceeds, so that this knowledge in itself is both the procession and the act of receiving its essence—*procedere in quantum imago est procedere cognoscendo eum a quo procedit, ita quod ipsa talis cognitio sit ipsa processio et acceptio suae essentiae.* Knowledge here constitutes being itself. This text from the *De intellectu et intelligibili* is further elucidated by a passage in the *De visione beatifica* in which Dietrich says that this emanation, by which the intellect emanates by essence from its principle, constitutes its conversion into its own principle—*ut ejus emanatio, qua intellectualiter emanat per essentiam a suo principio, sit ipsius in ipsum principium conversio.* These formulas must be understood in order to indicate here the intuition of a coincidence between two metaphysical movements which seem to be inverse—"the idea," as Bergson has said of another doctrine, "that the 'conversion' of the Alexandrians, when it becomes complete, makes it but one with their 'procession.'"

We cannot here engage in a comparison of our Domini-

can with his sources, but let us note the presence of
Augustine alongside Proclus and the Arabs. The active
intellect is not only identified with the *imago Dei,* but
with the hidden depths of memory (*abstrusa profunditas
memoriae*) in the hidden recess of the mind (*abditum
mentis*). In the possible intellect, Dietrich discovers a
less central, more external thought, the *exterior cogitatio.*
Aristotelian terms are converted into Augustinian expressions; they are utilized to treat of the union with
God and the interior life. Working in the midst of men
who, like the Thomists, considered the active intellect as
a faculty of the soul, a kind of accident, our Dominican
posits an intellect which is a substance, endowed with
even a certain causality with respect to the soul. Let us
cite—without comment—one text: "The active intellect
is the intrinsic causal principle of the soul"—*Intellectus
agens est principium causale animae intrinsecum.* It is,
in the life of the spirit, the vital principle, like the heart
in a living being—*sicut cor in animali.* For him it is
essential to our interior being; to conceive of it as unique
for all men, "separated," would be to destroy our highest
life. "Since the highest life of man consists in living intellectually, it is not at all likely that the interior principle
of this life—the active intellect—would not be, for each
one, his own possession and interior to him." The Arabs
are rejected. And each one of us sees himself possessing
a principle of coincidence with God. Let us use another
of Bergson's formulations: "When man, having emanated
from the divinity, comes to return to it, he perceives only
a unique movement where previously he had seen the
two opposite movements of going out and returning."
Dietrich of Freiberg no doubt constructed his theory of
the active intellect to assure us of a possibility of this sort.

To complete this succession of original figures, let us
discuss a layman, the Franciscan tertiary Ramon Lull.[11]

---

[11] Ramon Lull, born in Palma de Mallorca (Majorca) in 1232
or 1235, devoted his life after his "conversion" (1262) to the

A hermit and traveler, religious troubadour, logician, and apostle, this Majorcan has left a superabundance of works of all kinds. A learned Spaniard has very well said that "he improvised his systems like Lope de Vega his dramas." Latin was not the only language of his teaching; the major part of his works were written in Catalan, while some were immediately translated or perhaps even written in Arabic. A man of the frontiers of Christendom, he developed his thought with the Saracens in mind; some of whom, he thought, were well versed in philosophy. He disputed with their doctors, and it was one of their doctrines, Averroism, which he discovered and pursued in Latin lands, even to Paris, where he went to argue against the 219 propositions condemned in 1277. To convert the infidel and to train missionaries, he recommended the establishment of colleges for the study of Eastern languages, one of which he attempted to found at Miramar, on his native island of Majorca. Roger Bacon, too, had praised the knowledge of languages and proposed practical ends for his philosophy renewed by "experimental science." "I have considered philosophy," he had written to the pope, "according to the considerable utility it has for the conversion of the infidel; thanks to this science, those who cannot be converted will at least be restrained either by the works it allows to be accomplished, or by the war it makes it possible to conduct against them." Ramon Lull belongs to the same age and spirit of crusade or mission: he engaged in a dialectical war against the Saracens by propounding his *Ars magna* for Christendom.

This practical intention put aside, to what essential ideas does "the art of Lull" correspond? Some have treated with an amused interest the involutions in which

---

Crusade and the conversion of the infidel. From this fact both his doctrine and his travels to princes and popes and his missionary voyages to Africa were derived. He taught at Montpellier and then at Paris (1287-89, 1297-99, 1309-11). He died in 1316 while returning from a last missionary voyage during which he had been tortured.

he has cast his fundamental concepts, be they absolute or relative. We do not completely understand either their function or their role in the intellectual life; but we can state that in his work all knowledge is reduced to a combination of principles. "By an ordered mingling," he tells us, "of the principles themselves, it is possible to designate the secrets and the truths of nature"—*per ordinatam mixtionem ipsorum principiorum significantur secreta et veritates naturae.* Lull's imagery expresses the idea of a universal science. "Since each science possesses its own principles, different from the principles of the other sciences, the intellect requires and desires that there should be a general science with respect to all the sciences, with its own general principles, in which the principles of the other particular sciences would be enveloped and contained, as the particular in the universal." Bypassing genera without common traits, disciplines separated by their specificity, the *Ars magna,* to a greater extent than metaphysics or Aristotelian logic, seeks to realize the unity of knowledge. How was Lull able to think this unification possible? His project, Gilson has said, "has sense only in a system of knowledge and of the world as completely unified as that of the Augustinians of the thirteenth century." When considering Scripture, Roger Bacon spoke of a single wisdom; his *Opus majus* outlined an encyclopedia. As an example of their symbolism, St. Bonaventure wrote a short work on the way to reduce the arts to theology: *De reductione artium ad theologiam.* Ramon Lull moves in this symbolic universe, where every creature speaks of the Creator; we read in one of his mystic works: "A friend is asked: What is the world? He answers: For those who know how to read, it is a book in which one learns to know my Beloved." Could it not be said that the *Ars magna* unifies all human knowledge from the point of view of God? The absolute principles of knowing are indeed nothing but divine "dignities," such as goodness, grandeur, power, wisdom, glory.

Lull's intellectual technique is based on these eminently religious "blessed qualities"—*qualitates benedictae.*

Quite naturally, theology will make use of the *Ars magna,* will enter into the interplay of its necessities, and will prove the articles of faith against the infidel. "A universal religion, supported by an equally universal method of thinking, this," Bréhier has said, "is the idea Lull has of catholicity." His work is a continuation of Anselm's; in this connoisseur of Islam, the person of the infidel is made specific and asserts himself in the face of the Christian. To comprehend Lullism, it is necessary to imagine a mode of disputation in which "the Catholic prepares his adversaries for the comprehension of God and the interior acts of his dignities." Although well informed and reasonable, the Saracens in fact know very little about the divine essence and dignities; the Christian stands before him with the data of his belief. If he did not have faith, he would not be able to prove anything; after proof his faith will remain: "I propose," he says, "to prove in such a fashion that the condition of faith remains intact"—*Intendo taliter probare quod habitus fidei maneat integer.* In what do these proofs, encompassing even the Trinity, consist? They prevent thinking the contrary, the negation of the dogma: "I have proved," says Lull again, "the divine Trinity in such a manner that the human intellect cannot reasonably comprehend [that it does not exist]"—*probavi divinam trinitatem tali modo quod intellectus humanus non potest rationabiliter intelligere. . . .* A person understands the Trinity when he can refute his adversaries: "in as much as I have sufficient means to confound all the errors opposed to this dogma"—*in quantum habeam sufficientiam ad confundendum omnes errores contra ipsum.* If the proof is of the order of a refutation, we continue to think according to the manner of Anselm. E. Longpré has attempted to find the source of the "dignities" Lull attributes to God, and of the kind of argumentation that depends on them, in Richard of Saint-Victor: this hypothesis seems to be happily oriented. Despite the philosophical invasion which brings "Averroism," the tradition of Anselm and Richard is preserved, and is utilized to resolve problems posed for Christian thought by the Aristotelianism of the Arabs. This is the same conflict that is found running throughout the speculative diversity of the thirteenth century and for which Thomism was only *one* of the solutions.

Chapter V

JOHN DUNS SCOTUS AND WILLIAM OF OCKHAM

One scholar has contrasted John Duns Scotus to Thomas Aquinas as Kant to Leibnitz, the critic to the dogmatist. His purpose was to indicate the significance of Scotus's work, and to place it in the general perspective of the intellectual history of the Middle Ages: with the thirteenth century, the age of syntheses would have definitely passed; the historian ought to change his metaphor and speak of dissociation, of dissolution. We will have to modify somewhat this view of an age of criticism. At least when adopting Thomism as the center of reference, it would seem to be difficult to agree with Gilson that the condemnation of 1277 substituted a defensive attitude for the "effort to conquer philosophy by renovating it." Moreover, even when induced "by the solicitations of theology," a criticism of philosophy "by itself" is not the same as a criticism of philosophy by theology, and even in his criticism of the philosophers, the theologian can "create anew in the philosophical order." These expressions from the same historian indicate the nature of the problems Duns Scotus[1] and William of Ockham,[2] also a Franciscan, pose for the historian.

Duns Scotus will retain our attention for some time. Our "critical spirit" is a rather bad translation of his *subtilitas*, famous among the Schoolmen; it means a more complex manner of thinking, in which rigor tempers boldness without obstructing it. His writings allow us to witness attempts to prove, in long internal dialogues, concepts which he makes his own. His course is that of a searcher, not that of a doctrinaire; but after the materials have once been verified, the structure, as a steeple, follows —to prove and to construct are merely parts of the same activity. This attitude seems to me to be of great interest for us. Seen from our time, the Middle Ages appear as a period of naïve dogmaticism; modern philosophy looks in vain for criticism in it—hence the profusion of modern studies on medieval "theories of knowledge." It is often forgotten that, from age to age, men's attention is not directed toward the same objects. At the end of the eighteenth century, men speculated on the circumstances of the possibility of a mathematical science of nature. At the beginning of the fourteenth century, speculation had perhaps another center, namely: Under what conditions is a theology possible? It would then be necessary to look for the reflective aspect of medieval thought in its

[1] John Duns Scotus was born in Littledean (Scotland) about 1265 and studied at Oxford and Paris, dividing his life and his teaching between these two cities: Oxford, about 1300, 1305-06; Paris, 1302-03, 1304-05, 1306-07; sent to Cologne, he died there in 1308.

[2] William of Ockham was born in Surrey shortly before 1300. He studied at Oxford from 1312 to 1318 and lectured on the *Sentences* there from 1318 to 1320. Summoned to the Curia in 1324 to justify his teaching, he escaped from Avignon with the Franciscan general Michael of Cesena in 1328 and took refuge with the Emperor Louis of Bavaria. He then became engaged in the controversy over poverty and the conflict between the Empire and the Church—hence his political writings. He died in 1349 or 1350.

speculation on the science of God. Duns Scotus, for example, in the prologue—which we have already cited —of his *Opus Oxoniense* or, to use the title of the critical edition, of his *Ordinatio,* has written one of the finest of Western speculative texts.

Before discussing the possibility of a theology, we must take cognizance of its necessity. Let us go back to the early years of the fourteenth century, after the Aristotelian invasion. What good is it to speculate about Revelation, if reason alone is sufficient for everything? Such is the spirit of the philosophers: Aristotle, his Arabic disciples, and those who would want to follow them. When confronted with them, the theologian must justify his function. Duns Scotus bases his defense on the intellectual position of man: In a being that acts according to its knowledge, it is indispensable to determine the end toward which it tends and the means it has to attain it. Let us begin with this philosophical principle.

For the believer, the end of life is the vision of God— not the consideration of him in terms of one of those concepts the metaphysician forms beginning with the sensible, but to truly *see* him "face to face," in his supersensible reality. To *wish* an end, one must consider the attainment of it possible. Does our understanding know that it is capable of an intellectual intuition of God? It could if it already possessed a similar intuition about its own nature. But all our knowledge begins with sensation and is composed of what is abstracted from it; the only acts of knowing we experience relate to sensible objects or abstractions derived from them. Aristotle saw this fact and deduced from it his theory of the intellect; when suggesting that we are not capable of seeing an intelligible such as God, he only follows his reason—he is truly "the Philosopher." Avicenna, however, composes an objection; this philosopher does not conceive of the object proper to our understanding in the same way as Aristotle. According to Avicenna's definition, it would be *being,* in all its indetermination, whether sensible or not. Duns Scotus, who will make this thesis his own, asks himself if it is a purely philosophical position: Avicenna was a Moslem, he believed in immortality, he conceived of the human intellect in terms of a beyond where it could grasp the supersensible; with philosophy, he mingled his belief. In conclusion, "we must deny that we *naturally* know that being is the first object of our intellect, and this we hold because of the total indetermination of being for the sensible and the nonsensible"—*negandum, quod naturaliter cognoscimus ens esse primum objectum intellectus nostri, et hoc secundum totam indifferentiam entis ad sensibilia et insensibilia.* It is as a theologian that Duns Scotus must take up the view of Avicenna on the object of the understanding.

When discussing theories of the intellect, we have touched on this doctrine. Now it must be clarified, for it seems to be completely paradoxical: a reason naturally slighting itself; a theory of knowledge founded on a revelation. Our problem consists in suggesting a schematic picture of a doctrine still in the process of being elaborated when death interrupted the work of its propounder. It is possible to distinguish three stages in its development.

In the first, we consider reason completely free from all revelation; historically this situation has been realized in Aristotle. From the experience that all intellection ends with concepts, abstracted from the sensible, he concluded and could only conclude that the natural object of our intellect consists in "that which the thing gives to the senses" (*quidditas rei sensibilis*). From this point of view, the intuition of a pure intelligible would require us to leave our nature. Of Aristotelian man it cannot be said that he desires to see God. For him, this would be to wish the impossible. There is nothing within him to *demonstrate* this impossibility, but neither is there anything to indicate the opposite.

In the second stage, Christianity intervenes, from the outside, as "news." The same human nature appears to be capable of different states: before the Fall, today, immortal after the Resurrection. The humanity of Aristotle's theory corresponds to the lowest state of human nature, the consequence of Adam's sin. Within this perspective of history, Duns Scotus sees, between the Philosopher and himself, Revelation telling him that our intellect is capable of an intellectual intuition, even of God; he distinguishes the object which defines our intellect in experience, *pro statu isto,* from its object *ex natura potentiae:* the being of Avicenna. Reflection does not make us take possession of our nature; without divine Revelation, we are mistaken even about ourselves, unless we refuse to remain ignorant of our essence. Although his error was not strictly necessary, the Philosopher was in a situation offering him no escape; the theologian places himself on the outside. But because of this, he is not left without the wherewithal of a dialectic against philosophy; he does not stop with a recourse to faith.

In the third stage, Duns Scotus allows his adversary to formulate his objections in order to demonstrate that he contradicts himself and destroys his own argument. When he persists in enclosing us in the *quidditas rei sensibilis,* the strict Aristotelian forgets that he creates a metaphysics himself, a science that is determined by the same object as the Scotist intellect—indeterminate being, from that indetermination upon which universality is founded (meaning here a concept transcending the sensible as much as primary philosophy transcends physics). Metaphysics is a fact: the philosopher who practices it cannot reject its foundation in human nature, a foundation the theologian points out to him.

In his proofs of God, Scotus seems to be aware of this transcendence of metaphysics. He argues from efficient causality, but apropos of the Thomistic argument of the First Mover, the immobile principle of all the movement we observe, he remarks that one must be more a metaphysician to prove that he is the first, than a physician to prove that he is the mover. Since it is as a metaphysician that he must end, he will begin as one: however apparent it may be, movement is, after all, only a fact derived from the sensible and the contingent. It is better to build the necessary structure of the possible only on the properties of being. To begin, not with a given effect, but with the possibility of an effect (the *effectibile*), is to follow the most certain road toward the highest idea of God accessible to our speculations, and even this approach Duns Scotus questions when he asks if, among beings, there is an infinite existent in act: *Utrum in entibus sit aliquid actu existens infinitum?* With the idea of the infinite, we are at the heart of the whole problem of theology.

Theology is the science of God. Duns Scotus's idea of science suggests the influence of Robert Grosseteste and the mathematicism of Oxford. A thing is known when it is possible to demonstrate its properties as a geometer does with a triangle; a priori knowledge—*propter quid,* as the Middle Ages said—is scientific. To determine properties in this way, it is necessary to have a distinct idea of their subject—an intuition of its essence or an equivalent notion. According to the philosophers themselves, we lack this with respect to God. This is a serious deficiency; from indeterminate being, from the *ens in communi,* it would no more be possible to deduce what is proper to the divine essence than to derive the properties of a triangle from the concept of a figure. Let us note this pre-Cartesian feeling of the inadequacy of general ideas, this need for distinct, particular concepts. To know God, we cannot proceed *propter quid,* in a truly scientific fashion; we must reason *quia*—or as we would say, a posteriori. We must be content with a debased science. This is what has been done by metaphysicians who know God only by the effects of which He is the cause; the results they have obtained indicate that when reason alone is utilized the way is not sure. We are posterior to 1277, the year of the condemnation of the errors of the philosophers. For Christians there are two characteristics of the true God: his freedom and the Trinity. Beginning with sensible effects, Greco-Islamic metaphysics inferred opposing characteristics for its first cause and ended in error. This failure of pure reason extends to the end of man and the manner of arriving there; the philosophers, in fact, did not know that God as a cause is free from restraint, or that His essence is communicable to three persons—*Deus contingenter causans, Essentia communicabilis tribus.* They have not demonstrated their errors; this they were not able to do They have been "led," as it were, to deny these truths by the sensible experience that necessarily furnished them with their point of departure.

Arabic Peripateticism, so mingled with Neoplatonism, seems to be constantly present in the mind of Scotus. Since they conceive of but one necessary process coming out from the Principle, the philosophers envision only one equally necessary return. The theologian rejects this scheme: his God treats with complete freedom the beings He has freely created. The beatitude He promises us is seen as a gift; we cannot want it as if it were our due. We certainly must merit salvation, but our merits are only necessary and sufficient as a consequence of a divine decree: the Christian does not move toward his end according to a natural sequence, a necessary *processus.* His liberty subsists in the shadow of divine liberty. Between the two, Duns Scotus perceives an important connection. To prove, contrary to the philosophers' views, that God is free, the *Opus Oxoniense* infers from contingency, to "save" it as a datum in the world, a "primary contingency" in the principle of the world. This is to admit that, in cause and effect, contingency is not reduced to a privation, a simple lack of being, but constitutes a positive reality, a *modus positivus*—indetermination by the plenitude of a will, human or divine. At the very foundation of being, something escapes the necessity of natures, so dear to philosophy; the world becomes free for the human-divine history recounted by Scripture and into which the Christian life is thrust. But for Duns Scotus,

the liberty of God does not have a merely practical character; the same is also true of the Trinity. In the eyes of
this Franciscan, to love constitutes the supreme act. Now,
without faith in the Trinity, man is turned toward the
infinite essence, which is the sovereign good, as if it sub-
sisted only in one Person, whereas in its eternity, it is
communicated among three. The error of reason passes
into love, which loses its correctness of judgment, no
longer conforming to its object. Let us recall that Trinitarian speculation is not without ties to mysticism: we
will see that a certain manner of loving corresponds to
the *Essentia communicabilis tribus,* to the "communicability" or liberality that theology posits for the supreme
nature.

Let us summarize our discussion about freedom. Our
end appears as a Trinity freely giving itself. Beyond these
characteristics or "conditions" of the infinite essence, there
is no distinct knowledge of our end enabling us to arrive
there. If the characteristic of a religion is merit before
God, natural religion does not exist; if the task of a
morality is to determine the relationship between man and
the supreme being, natural morality is necessarily incomplete. Since reason perceives the impossibility of a
"philosophical salvation," and since Revelation is inter-
jected into nature, the theologian is philosophically justified in expounding it. This is the first aspect of the
philosophical introduction to theology which encompasses
the work of Scotus.

The metaphysical quest (*inquisitio metaphysica*), by
proving the existence of an infinite in being, furnishes
Scotus with the highest concept (*conceptus perfectissi-
mus*) which any human understanding, seeking His very
essence, can form of God—that of an infinite being. But
God is not only being, for he knows and he wills; to
know and to will are properties attributable to the
essence as well as to their subject. From this point of
view, we can apprehend the a priori (*propter quid*)
knowledge that is lacking in philosophy: God is seen in

himself as the subject for knowledge. This presupposes a distinction and an order between the divine essence and attributes comparable to those that exist between a subject and its properties; and this distinction and order interior to the divine nature make it possible to find there the foundation of the Trinity.

The Cartesian infinity will prohibit the distinction of anything within the divine simplicity; it will not allow even a distinction of reason—that is, in thought, as opposed to a distinction between realities—*ne quidem ratione*. The Scotist infinity, on the other hand, does not do away with either distinctions or order among being, knowing, and willing. Their real identity does not prevent a *formal* nonidentity (a famous Scotist expression). Eternity, on the other hand, excludes discussion in terms of time, but a kind of anteriority remains: it is possible to discern a logical order in the divinity, some nontemporal moments (these *instantia naturae* were famous in scholasticism). Conforming to these moments and in this order, the a priori knowledge of God that we do not have within ourselves is eternally realized in Him. This is the absolute state of theology—*theologia in se*—considered by itself, in its purity and fullness, before being communicated to any creature. Since, as we have said, the divine intellect does not find its object only in the infinite essence, but produces all the others as an infinity of second objects, theology in itself is universal knowledge. The Scotist doctrine of Ideas, joined to the notion of formal nonidentity, is the foundation of this conception of "theology as science." This knowledge realized in God transcends anything a finite mind could possible acquire; by a requirement to surpass that brings back to mind the *Proslogion,* the horizon of an infinite understanding extends to include *more* of the knowable than any other can naturally know, to the knowable that *He alone* can naturally know. A metaphysics that proves an infinite knowledge, as well as an infinite being, posits a "transmetaphysical" knowledge which only the Absolute possesses by nature, but which can be communicated by grace, in different degrees, if it, an object naturally hidden from all other minds, remains free to reveal itself (*objectum voluntarium*). Absolute knowledge, theology, and the God who reveals *Himself* share an evident connection or identification. Again we encounter, this time under its second aspect, the philosophical introduction to theology: the latter is always necessary, no longer relatively, for man in quest of Revelation, but absolutely, as the knowledge proper to the infinite being.

The function of the concept of infinite being in Scotus is to posit something beyond itself. The concept provides the ultimate end of the science of being as far as a notion of its Principle is concerned, but it does not constitute a science of God. If we must prove an infinite in being, it is because the proposition "the infinite being exists" is not self-evident for us. It would be self-evident, however, for a mind which acquires a distinct notion of deity; that is, the divine essence as such, in its singularity—*deitas, essentia ut haec*. These terms designate "the subject of theology in itself," in its transcendence with respect to metaphysics and even *our* theology. In the same way that a singular notion of God would show us His oneness, when the existence of "something infinite" has once been attained, the dialectic of Scotus must prove that there is only one. The idea of the infinite does not carry any more immediate evidence for oneness than for the existence of its object. Duns Scotus gives a certain validity to St. Anselm's argument only by transposing it into a proof for the infinity of an existent; as to the First (a vestige of Avicenna), having proven that He is possible by Himself and without cause, he concluded that He exists by Himself. The Scotist proofs do not proceed a priori from an idea of God—which, on the contrary, they construct as a result of their own development—but a posteriori, in a paradoxical style. The argument from the efficient cause does not begin with contingent facts, no matter how manifest (*ex contingentibus, tamen manifestis*), but places itself at first in the order of natures, essences, and possibilities (*de natura et quidditate et possibilitate*). From a given causality, only the possibility which it includes is retained—that of an effect (*effectibile*) in correlation to that of a cause (*effectivum*), which implies that of a *primum effectivum*—necessarily existent, as we have indicated. Arbitrary by beginning with the purely logical possibility of a concept, the passage from possible to actual being causes no difficulty in this unique case, provided it is a matter of departing from a possible *being* (*possibile reale*) such that it can be abstracted from a datum of fact. The pair *effectibile-effectivum* expresses an ontological structure like the pair "finite-infinite" to which it leads. The entire order of essences proceeds from a necessary existent, which Gilson says is not "infinite because it is" but is because it is infinite, since by surmounting "the obstacles of essence," Scotus discovers "something beyond essence."

Seeing in God the correlative of the finitude bestowed on us and on things, our idea of infinite being, a "privative concept," corresponds to our position in Creation, but the concept lacks the ability to make it completely precise. The metaphysical relationship of the finite to the infinite does not encompass the entire theological dependence (in the sense of revealed theology) of the creature with respect to the Omnipotent Creator, still less the specific relationship of the created mind to the Trinity of which it is the image. How, in fact, can the imitation be disclosed if one is ignorant of the model? In the dogma of the Trinity, faith posits a connection which is not self-evident for the reason that conceives its state. The latter is derived from natural light, since common revelation does not convey any particular notion about God comparable with the intuition of His essence. The theologian must become a metaphysician in order to elaborate the concepts that are applicable to the divine, from a generality embracing the infinite as well as the finite. The revealed data thus obliges metaphysics to become really "transcendent" knowledge, in the sense that the transcendence of being makes from it a concept valid both in God and in Creation. The work of the philosophical theologian will then be able to remove the apparent contradictions in dogma that a philosophy too closely connected with the sensible would point out. But Scotus seems to tend still further, to "proofs," by a complex examination whose ideal scheme can perhaps be represented as follows: Granted that faith presents us with the Trinity, our speculations find there an object of thought without internal contradiction, and they recognize the perfection of it. The adversary—that is to say, the philosopher who believes the contradictory dogma which slights the divinity —is refuted; to the believer, the same reasons make it seem absurd to renounce the idea born of his faith. A continuer of Anselm, Duns Scotus knows how to limit the scope of a theological proof; by explaining Richard of Saint-Victor, he explains himself: "even if there are necessary reasons, they are not evidently necessary"—*etsi sint necessariae rationes, tamen non sunt evidenter necessariae.* Necessity without evidence: the theologian remains a believer.

These necessary reasons presuppose an intellect that begins with the necessary, which proceeds *ex necessariis;* at the point of departure for our knowledge, facts and contingent connections are not sufficient, the contents of thought bound to necessity are needed—that is to say, essences. Since, in our present condition, everything begins with the senses, the intellect must extract *natures* from sensory data. This expression is Avicenna's; his logic and metaphysics teach us to conceive of an essence in a pure state (*natura tantum*). That of the horse, for example—*equinitas tantum*—is not confounded either with particular horses which alone exist, or with the general idea which our mind applies to them; between singularity and universality, it remains indeterminate (*natura indifferens*). From this point of view, Duns Scotus poses the classical questions in epistemology and ontology, the problems of universals and of individuation: How can the same nature become a general thought on the one hand, an individual thing on the other? Here we are not concerned with the constitution of the individual; let us merely see in nature, as a state of indifference, the idea communicating with the real. Being and unity go together; to every degree of being corresponds a degree of unity. Existence possesses the unity of the individual, or in scholastic terminology, the numerical unity—*unitas numeralis*. Pure unindividuated essence has a unity of its own, less than the numerical unity—*unitas minor unitate numerali*. With this famous expression, the universal acquires a distinct foundation within the singular. This nature, which comprises the content of our concept, is *found* by the intellect in sensory data. "To begin with the sensible" is usually interpreted as meaning "to know the singular first of all." In reality, Scotus tells us, the senses do not apprehend the singular as such; they stop with the indifferent. The Scotist intellect has no need to pass from the particular to the general, since the indetermination of natures enables them to be found in all their individuals; the indifference, and therefore the commonness, of these natures—*naturae communes*—assures the universality of their influence.

While it is clear that there is no "reduction" here which detaches the essences from the real to make them the pure object of an *Ego,* one is reminded of the phenomenology of Husserl. For systems of this type, experience never furnishes anything but examples. Crossing over, they grasp essences; the a priori is their climate. It is true that, as a theologian, Duns Sotus formulates necessary reasons about a God whose essence is not given to him. But he merely posits an intellect which conceives the *ens in communi;* such a notion does not contain the nature of any being and it does not constitute either a species or even a genus. It is not however unrelated to the *naturae communes* from which our mind has drawn it. This parentage seems essential: indeterminate though it may be, the *ens in communi* (which should not be translated "being in general": it means rather "the nature of being," common by indetermination, like every nature, and taken in itself, before it is effected by the generality which comes from the mind), possesses a definite content, in no way ambiguous. This is the doctrine of the *univocacy of being*— "This being that is nothing but being" (Gilson); an abstraction which cannot be reduced to a concept and can be treated like an essence: *natura entis;* and the Scotist essences are of the order of "the existable"; their science, metaphysics, is "real science." If it is applied to the divine, this is because of "transcendent" notions like that of univocal being: the perfections that are attributed to God are elevated to the same transcendence, above genera and finitude; treated as essences each of which remains itself, the Scotist attributes are not lost in the infinite. This is the doctrine of *formal distinction,* which is without any doubt the common bond of the Scotist school, whose unity seems to be derived less from common theses than from a mode of thinking, from the speculative technique which utilizes this famous distinction.

These are the conditions under which Duns Scotus, when confronted with the "philosophers," continued the investigations of Anselm and Richard. The fourteenth-century doctor placed his Avicennian-Oxonian disposition in the service of speculation; he knew in what his reasons consisted and on what they were founded. The views on divinity developed from them do not remain scattered in his work, but are organized in virtue of the ideal of a priori knowledge that we have seen realized in God. His constant analyses of the infinite thought and will give his theology the appearance of a "divine psychology." This word conveys the impression of boldness and arbitrariness that such constructions give. Duns Scotus, however, always inclines to an extreme rigor; how then can an expression be found which, after the lapse of six centuries, adequately characterizes his efforts? Let us recall the importance of the notion of essence. Divine acts, in his doctrine, are viewed as *intentions;* seeing the infinite essence

as their primary object, the divine intellect and will constitute the Trinity. Then the way in which they "pass" to
secondary objects is determined; the theologian thus imitates in his discourse that which is, in itself, only intuition,
evidence—but ordered evidence, *evidentia ordinata.* In
all these characteristics, the theology of Scotus resembles
an attempt at "phenomenology," not of the human conscience, but of the Absolute. Beginning with the infinite
essence, it is concerned with describing how, by acts of
knowing and loving, a living God, a Creator and Saviour
of other beings, constitutes Himself. By revealing *Himself,*
the trine and free God calls us to this speculative task
(which is also enjoined by the love that saves); but in
order to undertake it, an intellect that moves in the realm
of essences is necessary. The realism of the *naturae communes* establishes the possibility of metaphysics, the discipline of the *natura entis,* the instrument of theological
exposition.

In histories of philosophy the French Franciscan Pierre
d'Auriol [3] appears in the company of Durand of Saint-
Pourçain as a precursor of the nominalism of William of
Ockham. But he hardly merits this role. He deserves a
different place due to the originality of his work. An extensive and precise knowledge of earlier doctrines, discussion and exposition characterized by considerable clarity,
constant return to several synthetic views, and extreme
conscientiousness—these are one's first impressions of his
Commentary on the Sentences. Duns Scotus is criticized at
length, especially for his analysis of the Trinity and his
theory of the *natura communis:* the real is not, in any
degree, indifferent; there is then no need to explain that it
becomes, as it were, singular. "To seek that by which a
thing, existing outside the intellect, is singular, is to seek
nothing"—*quaerere aliquid, per quod res, quae extra in-*

[3] Pierre d'Auriol(e) was born in the environs of Gourdon. He
studied in Paris in 1304 and taught at Bologna (1312), Toulouse (1314), and Paris (1317-20). Named archbishop of Aix
in 1321, he died in 1322.

tellectum est, est singularis, est nihil quaerere. By declaring the search for a principle of individuation to be in vain, Auriol does not completely dispense with discussion of this subject. The coherence of his speculations on individuality is not, however, immediately apparent; the problems seem to be displaced rather than removed. In the realm of the mind, we find not a little complexity in what has been called his "conceptualism." This word may be kept by restricting its meaning: it merely indicates the negation of the realism of the Scotist natures—the refusal to admit, in the individual, this *distinct* basis for the universal. Let us also note that terms like *concipere, conceptio, conceptus* evoke a theme to which our theologian often returns; and that he says he follows Aristotle against Plato for the purpose of rejecting Ideas for the benefit of concepts. But as in all Aristotelianism, it must be asked what he keeps of the Platonism he rejects.

Auriol always deals with essences that are identified with specific natures. Instead of Avicenna's *equinitas tantum,* with which he is familiar, Pierre d'Auriol prefers a different example and another expression: *rosa simpliciter* —*the* rose, in the absolute sense, and not *the* roses in particular that are individuals. The adverbs *tantum* and *simpliciter* are important; while both indicate the purity of essences, the first suggests a relative indetermination, the second an absolute of plenitude. Pierre denies that the *Idea* of the rose, in which all roses "participate," exists except in the mind; the mind not only sees it, but gives it being by conceiving of it. But there is still a relationship of participation between the content of this concept and individual realities. By treating Auriol as an empiricist, it has been forgotten that for him the object of thought contains more than can be realized in things: truth does not consist in a conformity of the mind with the real; the relationship must be returned. Things are true according to the degree of their fidelity to their nature, which exists only in thought: "The truth of a thing is nothing but its essence; to be true is merely to follow the proper essence;

but no essence is subsisting"—*Veritas rei nihil aliud est quam ejus quidditas; nec esse verum est aliud quam assequi propriam quidditatem; nulla autem quidditas est subsistens.* The concept preserves the regulating power of the Idea over beings; the mind always apprehends essences and their necessity. This intellectual position is perfectly clear: Plato was wrong to posit a realm of multiple intelligibles, a "forest of natures" (*sylva naturarum*). Let us suppose, on the contrary, that all essences subsist, but only by becoming one: we have then the very being of God, whose plentitude simply condenses, as it were, in Himself the entire world of intelligibles: "Let someone imagine every entity subsisting in this way [as pure essence], by this fact he apprehends the Deity [that which God is]"—*Si ergo quis imaginetur omnem entitatem sic subsistentem, habet utique deitatem.* Consequently, created things are only imitations, reductions—that is, diminuated entities (*entitates diminutae*). Our concepts are true to the degree that, as notions of essences, they imitate the supreme essence, in as much as the Deity is their exemplary cause—*isti conceptus veri sunt inquantum a Deitate exemplati sunt.* By assuring the equilibrium of our "conceptualism," the Augustinian notion of a first truth saves the spirit of Plato. There is only one Idea, but it is sufficient, and equivalent to the entire intelligible world: the God of Pierre d'Auriol is this Idea conscious of itself; this supposed nominalist thus gives himself the right to reason as though Platonism were true, and he does not neglect to do so.

According to this perspective, all essences are founded in a single essence; divinity does not admit of internal division either in reality or in thought, *nec re nec ratione:* the basis of the Scotist exposition of the Trinity is ruined. Auriol cannot fail to utilize another theory; the spirit of Anselm and of Richard is found in his *Commentary on the Sentences,* assisted by a different technique than that of Scotus. Our Franciscan rejects the Thomistic formula: *articula fidei principia theologiae;* in theology dogmas do not hold the place of principles, but rather of conclusions. Not that it is a question of demonstrating them in a manner which would force philosophers or pagans to assent; the aim is merely to explain (*declarare*) the object to which one adheres by faith, to make an intellectual representation of it, a sort of nonsensory image (*imaginari per intellectum*).

In the course of this exposition, the theologian finds truths plainly demonstrable by natural reason, but which were unknown to the philosophers: "It is a fact that the divinely revealed Scriptures compel us to hunt for and to seek many truths that can, however, be deduced from propositions known by natural light. And if Aristotle had had these same occasions for research, he would doubtlessly have been more adequately lifted up to these objects"—*Constat enim quod scriptura divinitus revelata cogit ad venandum et inquirendum multa vera quae nihilominus necessario ex propositionibus sequuntur notis in lumine naturali. Et si Aristoteles habuisset occasiones hujusmodi, non dubium quod ad eas multo excellentius ascendisset.* An extremely interesting text, for "the spirit of medieval philosophy" as well as for the idea of "Christian philosophy" it reveals. Inside a theology and under its influence, metaphysics expands without shattering its nature. To Auriol's conceptualism we can apply his own psychology of the metaphysical theologian: to explain and to represent in the intellect the Trinity we do not see, an image must be available from which conclusions about the model will be drawn. Our soul will be this image. Between the *De trinitate* of Augustine and our author there is the *Monologion* and its demand for proof; Pierre selects for his point of departure: *mens, notitia, amor*—mind, knowledge, love. Let us consider the second term: "knowledge"; the concept of man will correspond with the divine Word. In this correspondence, our conceptualism finds greater rigor and sense.

By knowing itself, the Augustinian soul comes, as it were, *before* itself, in the capacity of an *object*. As knowl-

edge of the mind by the mind itself, however, the resulting *notitia* shares with the *mens* a single *essentia*. This
same essence subsists only according to two modes or, in
other words, in two different situations: first of all *in itself,*
then *before itself—in se, ante se*. With respect to the unity
of essence and the diversity of modes, the same situation
exists in God: the Word is the divinity as *object,* the Deity
posited in terms of the mode of being which consists in
being seen—*Deitas posita in esse prospecto*. Between the
Father and the Son, there is, as it were, no variation other
than this manner of being. The "consubstantiality" of the
divine Persons becomes clearer to us if we note that, in
the knowledge of itself, the soul is divided into two parts
by an interplay of relationships which does not alter the
absolute character of its essence. How can this be established? By showing that the object of all knowledge, *before* our mind, merely contains, under a new mode of
being, the essence of the thing that subsists *in* itself. With
an astonishing virtuosity, Pierre d'Auriol undertakes this
task: he wants a rigorously demonstrated Trinitarian psychology; this is indeed a case of philosophy inside a theology. The demonstration begins with an experience, the
familar example of *the* rose: "For it is a fact that the
intellect is directed to *the* rose and it experiences what is
placed before it in the capacity of an object"—*Constat
enim quod intellectus fertur super rosam simpliciter et
experitur illam sibi objeci objective*. We think natures,
almost Ideas. In these universals, we grasp the reality
of individuals, and even what they are: "In effect, the
person who conceives of the rose has in his intuition the
experience of something absolutely one, of which it can be
said that it is a thing exactly the same as the particular
roses existing outside the mind"—*Concipiens enim rosam
experitur in suo intuitu aliquid unum simpliciter, de quo
constat quod est res omnino eadem rosis particularibus
quae sunt extra*. This is an excellent example of the structure of medieval speculation: reflection is enclosed in the
framework of a theology; the experience of a concept is

referred to a doctrine of the Word, the "divine concept"; Platonic participation does not fully explain the relationship of the concept to the thing; the "consubstantiality" of the World with the Father must be considered. When William of Ockham encountered this extraordinary conceptualism, he rejected it.

To define the thought of William of Ockham, doctrinal history has taken over from the scholastic tradition the term "nominalism." We will attempt to find a precise meaning for it but without thinking that the problem of universals furnished Ockhamism with its central task. When he poses this question with respect to the knowledge that we can have of God, the English Franciscan points out that many things he has said or will say in the development of his commentary on the *Sentences* depend on the solution; by beginning with five of his questions devoted to the nature of the universal, our analysis again encounters the same group of problems we found in Scotus and Pierre d'Auriol with respect to the theory of the *naturae communes.* But we will be introduced to a new mode of thought.

Some of Ockham's views will remind us of certain opinions of Abelard, although no direct relationship between these "nominalisms" can be established. We should simply bear in mind that, from the twelfth to the fourteenth century, in spite of the metaphysics of the thirteenth century, men had in common a basic intellectual formation, based on the logic of Aristotle, Porphyry, and Boethius— in short, the instrument of and the apprenticeship in learning, the foundations for mental discipline. Universals were always discussed by writing a *de generibus et speciebus.* These genera and species that divide the Aristotelian world are for the intellect *praedicabilia,* possible predicates. In effect, all knowledge is resolved into propositions; propositions are resolved into terms, that is into subjects and attributes; the universal is defined as a possible attribute for several subjects. Propositions and terms are sometimes given in writing, sometimes spoken and understood, and sometimes merely thought—*in scripto, in voce, in mente.* But thought, like language, is developed and broken down: it is a kind of natural and universal interior language. Within the proposition, the term has a meaning; as a sign it is related to the thing whose place it takes— the relationship expressed by the verb *supponere (pro).* The "logic of the moderns," codified by Peter of Spain, completed the ancient *Organon,* the substance of the "old" and the "new" logic of the twelfth century; Ockham formulates the problem of universals by beginning with the theory of the *suppositio.*

By means of an example, let us return to the logico-grammatical atmosphere in which William of Ockham lived and in which his thought developed. Let there be *in voce* three propositions: *homo est vox dissyllaba, homo currit, homo est species* ("man is a two-syllable word," "man runs," "man is a species"). What represents the subject in each case? In the first, the very sound that makes the word: this is the *suppositio materialis.* In the second, one of the real, individualized things it represents: the *suppositio personalis.* In the third, something common to these individuals, *aliquod commune:* this is the *suppositio simplex.* This *aliquod commune* is the substance for the problem of universals. Here, the logician cedes his place to the metaphysician: "Whether this common thing is real or is not real, is of no importance to the logician, but it does matter to the metaphysician"—*Utrum autem illud commune sit reale vel non sit reale, nihil ad logicum, sed ad metaphysicum.* It is a question of knowing what kind of reality, what degree of being, the term "man" aspires to in the *suppositio simplex:* Is it something outside the mind, or only in the mind? Ockham classifies the doctrines that give the universal reality outside the mind (*extra animam*) according to the greater or lesser stability they grant it. When he comes to existence only in the mind (*tantum in anima*), he must choose between a real quality of this substance and a mere object of thought, something imaginary: must universals be posited in the mind as in their subjects or merely with the name of objects— *subjective in anima an objective tantum?* The psychology of the concept still moves among modes of being. *Beginning with the logic of language, the nominalist consciously sets up ontological problems.*

The last question permits a choice between three hypotheses, all of which are probable, concerning the nature of the concept. The conclusion of previous questions was that the universal has no reality *extra animam.* Evidence for this is found in the refutation of realism, all forms of which, one after another, are shown to be absurd. As in Abelard, an affirmation is derived from these negations and is made precise: the position of an absolutely singular, indivisible reality. Let us grant, to begin with, the maximum reality to the universal: this will be *a* thing; and the individual in which it is realized, *an* other; between the *two,* there would be a "real distinction." The individuals of a species are multiple; two possibilities are suggested for the specific nature: it can either remain one for all and unchangeable; or it can be multiplied, varying from one to the other, as the part with the whole. In the first case, the universal is enclosed, as it were, in itself: there is merely one more individual. Ockham represents Platonism in this way. In the second hypothesis, the universal must change into a singular: the singularity of the whole includes all the parts with an equal force. This same principle of homogeneity goes against a third thesis, expressing the true thought of Duns Scotus, of which the first two were erroneous interpretations. When properly understood, the *natura communis* of Scotus does not in any sense lay claim to the unity of the individual; between the one and the other, there is no room for a real distinction, but only for a formal one; in this way the nature can preserve its indifference.

Ockham sees all these nuances, but holds that distinctions of this kind—the degree of unity and of indifference —are absurd: he continues to posit a being in all respects equal to itself. In the reality of distinct things, there is no possible way in which one can be more indifferent than another, or numerically greater than another—*nec sunt possibilia quaecumque a parte rei qualitercumque distincta, quorum unum sit magis indifferens quam reliquum, vel quorum unum sit magis unum numero quam reliquum.* The real appears immediately and entirely singular; the principle of individuation becomes useless. It has been justly remarked that this position was not new; we have found it in Pierre d'Auriol, and Duns Scotus already knew it, only to reject it. When the singular no longer requires an explanation, the possibility of the universal must still be developed, to establish it in reality itself. If Socrates did not really have a greater relationship with Plato than with an ass, the notion of man would not be more adequately verified by Socrates and Plato than by Socrates and the ass. Thus genera and species are not purely fictive; as in realism, nominalism recognizes their foundation in reality, but conceives of it differently. Comparing Socrates and Plato to Socrates and the ass, the realists deduce: "There is a greater agreement between these beings . . . , therefore they agree in some nature"—*Est major convenentia . . . , ergo conveniunt in aliqua natura.* Ockham, however, says: "There is greater agreement between Socrates and Plato than between Socrates and this ass; it is not because of something which distinguishes them in some way that these beings are in agreement, but because in themselves they are in greater agreement"—*Est major convenientia inter Socratem et Platonem quam inter Socratem et istum asinum; non propter aliquid aliquo modo distinctum, sed seipsis plus conveniunt.* The realist makes the agreement of beings a community of nature, participation in one single essence, conceivable by itself; the nominalist leaves individuals completely undivided: the resemblance expressed by the concept moves from the whole of one to the whole of the other. This was to take up Abelard's position. Nominalism rejects the reality of a *distinct* foundation for the universal.

We have left both the real distinction and the formal distinction behind us: the Schoolmen still recognize the distinction from reason. The last chance for realism, the *natura communis* no longer has actuality in the core of the individual; while some would place it there as a potentiality, it is actualized and distinguished only by our understanding. But even these reservations do not satisfy Ockham. By definition, the singular denies the possibility that constitutes the universal *in potentia*. Between being able to be attributed to several subjects and not being able to be attributed to several subjects (the logical definition of the singular), there is a contradiction—*Posse praedicari de pluribus et non posse praedicari de pluribus contradicunt*. One contradictory statement does not include the other, but excludes it; the individual, the real repels all shadow of universality from itself. Universals are reduced to concepts, as exterior to things as the words that we utter about them. The universal *is* not *in* the thing any more than the word "Man" *is in* Socrates or *in* the things that it denotes—*universale non est in re non plus quam haec vox Homo est in Socrate vel in illis quod significat*.

The universal then is a sign and nothing more. Ockham's nominalism consists in holding firmly to this position. Where historians see anticipations of his doctrine —in Pierre d'Auriol, for example, and Henry of Harclay, chancellor of Oxford University—Ockham himself still saw realism and its absurdity. The conceptualism of the first rejects the division of the individual demanded by the Scotist nature; the general idea, however, contains that which things are: despite its universality, "the rose" that is thought is identified with particular roses. For Scotus, the *natura communis* constitutes a degree of being and an object of thought; for Auriol, it is merely an object of thought. In both cases, the problem turns on *essences,* distinct from things but nevertheless identical with them. William of Ockham denies the existence of these essences. He pursues the same absurd identity of the real and the universal in the teaching of Henry of Harclay. This

Oxonian master clearly saw that to posit a reality is to
constitute an individual: everything posited outside the
mind is by that fact singular—*omnis res posita extra
animam est singularis eo ipso.* But after this felicitous beginning, he develops his thought less happily. For Henry,
the singular engenders in the intellect a knowledge with
two degrees: a distinct notion expressing the proper noun;
a confused notion, represented by the common noun. In
the proposition "Socrates is a man," the subject and attribute are a single being; Socrates, in his absoluteness, *is*
Socrates even if confusedly conceived—*Socrates absolute
est Socrates ut tamen confuse conceptus.* The universal
would be derived from the singular, seen in a certain way.
One might as well say that according to the inclination of
our mind, a man would become an ass! Henry of Harclay
speaks as a realist who identifies the universal with the
singular. Ockham seeks a radical distinction between the
two. "If there is no essence distinct from existing singulars, the universals are related to being as signs which are
no more things than nouns themselves are the realities
which they designate."

The word "thing" (*res*) thrusts us into a completely
logical, colorless world. Everything is an individual. Let
us strip this last term of all sensory illusions; only abstract
properties remain. Here we are confronted with the problem of distinctions, so important in scholastic technique,
and which will be encountered again in Descartes's *Principia.* Ockham deals with it not only with respect to universals and the singular, but again in his discussion of the
attributes and being of God. In theology, he rejects both
the formal distinction of the Scotists and the distinction
from reason utilized by the Thomists among others. The
rejection of these distinctions implies a "criticism of abstraction," if "to abstract" means "to think of by itself
something that cannot be given by itself." Ockham foreshadows Hume by saying: "All that is discernible is different and all that is different is separable" (Laporte). But
here the negation of all distinction not implying separabil-

ity is a metaphysical thesis linked to a theology. For the logician, distinction signifies nonidentity. When two things *a* and *b* are not exactly identical, statements of the order "*a* is identical to *a*," "*b* is not identical to *a*" are verified. Inversely, when we have two contradictory statements, we cannot identify their subjects: from the opposition between propositions, it is possible to infer the distinction between beings. *Contradictio est via potissima ad probandam distinctionem rerum*—"Contradiction is the most efficacious method for proving the distinction of things." In this way, only one kind of distinction is ever attained; the point of departure, the opposition of contradictions, does not admit of degrees. All contradictions are equally repugnant—*omnia contradictoria habent aequalem repugnantiam.* Between "ass" and "not ass," "God" and "not God," "being" and "non-being," Ockham finds an equal repugnance which, since the terms of our propositions are signs, presupposes a homogeneous distinction, called "real," in being. Logic and ontology are joined. *Distinctio vel non identitas:* the nonidentity of one thing with another is as real as its identity with itself, as this interior indistinction that makes it the same—*eadem res.*

From the point of view of a thing understood in this way, to posit from its position some other is equivalent to not positing it in the first place; no act, not even a divine act, could establish the real subjects of two contradictory predicates in the position of one single existent. Here ontology reveals a vigor which will not be diminished by theology; as far as the horizon of His power extends, the God of Ockham would not know how to posit a thing and at the same time not posit it. To return to the example of universals, let us say that He could very well not create any of the individuals who constitute the world, but that once created in the singularity that we have established, none of these beings can, even through divine power, become common to others—*nec per potentiam divinam potest communicari.* It is bound to this ontology that one must see the theology of the Power that alone answers the question, Where can the power be found that is capable of making one of the terms of a real distinction exist without the other? In a theology which attributes to the Almighty the power to do all that can be done without contradiction, there is nothing contradictory in separating what is not bound by identity. God, if he had so desired, could have created one thing alone—it makes no difference which one—presently given with others. Ockham did not invent this thesis; he notes that before him (among the Franciscans) the possibility of matter subsisting without form had been deduced. He himself, however, utilizes this "common principle" to such an extent in physics, and even in logic, that both his age and ours have considered it as one of the principles of the systematic unity of his doctrine. This was to indicate a historical situation. *Est divinae potentiae attribuendum:* one *must* attribute to God a power which is limited only by a manifest contradiction. With this theme of absolute divine freedom, William of Ockham opposed a principle of Arabic Aristotelianism: a God who acts according to the necessity of nature. Continuing the movement of a Christian reaction marked by the condemnation of 1277, his teaching appears as "a believer's philosophy." So much the more so since he bases omnipotence on an article of faith, *Credo in Deum omnipotentem,* which he holds to be philosophically indemonstrable. But this pure theology is not merely articulated with a pure logic, valid only on the level of terms; the interplay of identity and exclusion extends to being itself, with an autonomous force: a summary metaphysics perhaps, but a vigorous one. If, by "thing," we understand *that* which cannot be divided, but which could very well exist by itself, nominalism can be seen as an ontology of the thing in which a logic of language mingles with a theology of omnipotence.

Being "separable from every other absolute" (no created relationship has its own reality), this property of things—*passio theologica*—is taken up by the theologian who considers them creatures or rather "creatables," as the Creator *sees* them. We emphasize the word "sees." If there is no essence distinct from beings—common natures, divine intelligibles, Ideas—it would be possible to conceive of knowledge in God only as an *intuition,* identical with His being, having for its objects both His own and every other reality, including the whole realm of the possible, extending as far as His powers of realization—*posse facere.* Here, the equation of knowing and being is less the result, it could be said, of an absolute *knowledge* than of an absolute *experience* in which each of the objects—*primo diversa, creata de novo*—is seen with a radical originality, in the novelty of its creation. The Ockhamist denial of essences finds here its meaning and its limitation: every entity distinct from the existing, not the entire necessary structure of the latter, is denied. The proposition "man is an animal" certainly does not refer back to an eternal archetype. It can only refer to something existing, and this cannot be, in the theologian's universe, the eternity of the human species according to Aristotle and Averroës; in the contingency of the created, the necessity of the assertion does not disappear, it becomes hypothetical: "if man is, man is an animal."

And the nominalism of concepts does not prevent, as we know, their universality. In this world where the distinction between necessary truths and contingent truths exists, the invocation of the divine omnipotence—*potentia Dei absoluta*—allows the dialectical proof that separates the accidental from the essential in the object of an investigation: valid predicables as well as things are both still admitted. Ockham, as we shall see, treats justifying grace in this way; his analysis of knowledge (abstract, intuitive, experimental) is developed in this context. Seen in this way, it does not imply the skepticism which some have thought they found in it by comparing the *potentia absoluta* with the mischievous spirit of Descartes.

According to his contemporary, the author of the *Tractatus de principiis theologiae,* Ockham's second "principle" is a maxim that he did not invent but which is associated with his name: *pluralitas non est ponenda sine necessitate ponendi*—"Plurality need not be posited unless it is necessary to posit it." The doctors of the thirteenth century moved in a world of entities that their fourteenth-century critic finds needlessly multiplied: essence distinguished from existence; relationships which claim a reality other than the absoluteness of their terms; intermediate species between the faculty of knowing and the exterior object; powers of the soul distinct both from its substance and its acts; the active intellect and the possible intellect—so many victims of the terrible Franciscan and his requirement of economy (although he was not exclusively responsible). The idea of simplicity, Aristotelian in origin, has no metaphysical connotations here: it implies only the rigor of a mind which does not wish to advance without compelling proof. Let us not put the principle of the economy of thought on the same plane as the principle of omnipotence, which is master in ontology: what is a rule for our intellect, is not in any sense meant for divine action. God often does by a greater number of means what He could do by fewer— *Frequenter facit Deus mediantibus pluribus quod potest facere mediantibus paucioribus*. The theologian is confronted with a first cause to which second causes, dispensable because of the omnipotence of the first cause, are added. Since it does not correspond to any necessity, second causality cannot be deduced, but William of Ockham posits it in a world created with superabundance. For the historian, Ockham's God provides the living antithesis of the God of Malebranche and Leibnitz, who will act in the simplest ways. The principle of economy does not enable us to rediscover a priori the divine configuration of the orders of nature and grace; it does remove human imaginings and leaves us with facts, derived from experience or revealed by Scripture.

Although Ockham's criticism strikes other masters, it is aimed principally at Duns Scotus when it deals with problems about God: the exposition of dogmas or natural theology—what Scotus called the *inquisitio metaphysica de Deo*. The Scotist foundation for this metaphysical quest disappears with the nominalistic rejection of the *naturae communes*. These essences abstracted from sensory data for the purposes of a priori speculation can no longer be seen as examples. Instead of building on the *natura entis*, the metaphysician can signify all data by using only the univocal idea of being. When he would prove the existence of God, he will not argue about the possible and its necessary constitution, but about the real and the manner in which it conserves itself. Experience reveals causes and effects to us; since an infinite series of simultaneous causes is impossible, the conserving causes of a given effect are finite in number. The conservation of things, which Ockham emphasizes, presupposes a first efficient cause, hierarchically above all its effects—*primum efficiens, nobilius omni effectu*. The primacy reached at the end of this demonstration is not such that it is possible to demonstratively conclude from it the oneness of this "first." In the attempt to reach God, the Ockhamist proof stops on this side of Scotus's proof; it revives a thesis anterior to the latter: the monotheism of the first article of faith—*Credo in unum Deum*—is indemonstrable. It may be said that for Scotus "being" implies an a priori power of position with respect to an order of essences, while for his critic it means a datum without dynamism. However, the demonstrative character of the proofs of God does not seem, in the fourteenth century, to have been contested only by the nominalists.

In retrospect, one can clearly see what becomes of the God of theology in a nominalistic mode of thought that knows only the real distinction. Since the unity of the divine being excludes all multiplicity of things, one is confronted with a radical indivisibility: an indistinct perfection both in reality and for thought—*una perfectio indistincta re et ratione*. "The divine attributes do not correspond to essentially, formally distinct perfections";

they are only diverse signs for the same thing. In contrast to the theologians of the thirteenth century, the Fathers whom Peter Lombard follows spoke only of divine *names* —*non posuerunt distinctionem nisi in nominibus et unitatem in re significata.* Through the Master of the Sentences, the nominalism of the fourteenth century communicates here with that of the twelfth. As a corollary, in this given simplicity, it is not possible to discern different levels; at every opportunity Ockham rejects as absurd the order that Duns Scotus establishes in God. From it, the "divine psychology" which constitutes Scotist theology was derived. Even when revealed, the Absolute does not admit of explanation: Ockham in opposition to Scotus posits an abyss of simplicity in which our analysis can no longer find anything to grasp.

When understanding and will are both founded in the completely simple divine essence, their distinction can no longer furnish, as in Henry of Ghent and Scotus, a point of departure for an explanation, if not a proof, of the Trinity. Is it even possible to state this truth of faith without the appearance of contradiction? From the premises "the Essence is the Son," and "the Father is not the Son," a theologian does not conclude, "then the Father is not the Essence"; he holds the opposite, "however the Father is the Essence." To put themselves in accord with logic, the Scotists introduce formal distinctions, which for Ockham clarify nothing; he thinks the formal distinction is no easier to hold than the Trinity of persons with a unity of essence—*non credo distinctionem formalem faciliorem ad tenendam quam trinitatem personarum cum unitate essentiae.* The Trinity appears to be a contradiction; reason finds nothing in its nature to remove the difficulty and advance into the mystery. Confronted with this impenetrable datum, the mind stops in a pure and simple faith. A similar criticism seems to extend to the *fides quaerens intellectum,* by putting an end to all speculative theology.

There are many resources in an Aristotelian tradition:

when an object escapes knowledge, dialectic remains. Evidence and necessity are inaccessible; if one still wants to reason in any case, one will seek probabilities capable of persuading. Hence all the nuances that can be observed in the attitudes of nominalist theologians on Trinitarian questions. For example, tradition tells us that the Son was *begotten* and that the Spirit *proceeds;* how is generation to be distinguished from procession? Duns Scotus, without too much difficulty, bases this distinction on the nonidentity of the understanding and the will. In the Ockhamist divinity, completely the same within itself, no reason for diversity can be found. Ockham however advances one, the inadequacy of which he notes. His great fifteenth-century disciple, Gabriel Biel, who takes up the same position without any greater illusions, explains that the master did not wish to be deficient in his role as a theologian; he wanted to satisfy professional honor. *Cum tamen turpe sit theologo non posse credendorum qualemcumque intellectum et rationem dare. . . .* "Is it not a disgrace for a theologian not to indicate some understanding and reason with respect to the things he must believe?"

Other theologians of the fourteenth century, the Dominican Robert Holkot and the Augustinian general, Gregory of Rimini,[4] declared the task impossible: the first refuses to add anything to the formulas of Trinitarian faith. The reserve of the second was violently criticized by Pierre d'Ailly: the very dignity of faith demands that it be accompanied by dialectic. "Our faith," says the celebrated nominalist, "is true and exceedingly salutary; it would therefore not be fitting if it were neither defended nor upheld by probable arguments"—*Fides nostra est vera et saluberrima, et per consequens inconveniens esset quod non posset defendi et probabiliter sustineri.*

---

[4] A few dates: Robert Holkot taught at Cambridge and died in 1349; Gregory of Rimini spent about ten years teaching at Paris beginning in 1341; he died in 1358. Gabriel Biel, who taught at Tübingen, died in 1495.

Trinitarian speculation is an essential tradition in the Church; the study of faith—*studium fidei*—must be maintained. An attempt will be made to represent something of what one believes, to make it appear true—*imaginari, apparere sic esse*. A certain representation of probabilities, Anselm's ideal still lives on among Ockhamists, although the means of realizing it seem feeble to us.

The sketch given above of the intellectual character of William of Ockham would remain too incomplete if some indication of his practical attitude were not added. Later we will speak of his conception of justifying grace. If, in his eyes, the whole order of salvation is a manifestation of the sovereign freedom of God, this sovereignty does not destroy nature, or its consistency and validity in its own order. Gilson has recently noted that natural ethics, founded on right reason and experience, constituted one "of the most certain" sciences for Ockham; and G. de Lagarde has shown the force that the idea of natural law had for him. Such statements are astonishing only to those who would deduce from an idea, if not a passion, of the divine power an entire doctrine, more complex and with greater equilibrium. His "nominalism," as we know, does not imply any basic skepticism with respect to concepts, universals, or the necessary; the genius of its author is no doubt found in "the coincidence of philosophical interests and religious interests without any common origin." Some of these interests are seen in the political writings of his last twenty years, polemical works in which weighty argumentation mingled with invective is expressive of considerable emotion. In them, the formidable Franciscan especially inveighs against the theocratic thesis according to which the Sovereign Pontiff would have received from Christ a fullness of power (*plenitudo potestatis*) giving him in the temporal as well as in the spiritual order a right to command limited only by natural law and revelation. If he invokes the traditional idea of the evangelical law as a law of freedom (*lex libertatis*) he does so without "anarchism," by recognizing that it imposes a certain yoke on men, but one that is lighter than that of the old Law. "Evidently the Christian law does not admit of a servitude as great as the Mosaic Law. But if the Pope, through the precept and disposition of Christ possessed a fullness of power such that rightly and without exception, his competence in the temporal and the spiritual extends to all that is not opposed to either divine law or natural law, the Christian law would be a law of terrible servitude, incomparably greater than that of the old Law." To understand the freedom of the Christian "negatively," to conceive of a right of the Franciscan Order or of the Empire to oppose pontifical decisions, is for Ockham simply to remind the theocrats of the limitations of all human power, to prohibit the use of the authority of Christ against the rights and freedoms (*jura et libertates*) that their fellow men have from nature and from God himself, to ask them finally how the Vicar of Christ can hold a supreme temporal power from the Saviour who had refused it for Himself by taking on humanity, suffering, and death (*homo passibilis et mortalis*). The same spirit animates his defense of both poverty and the independence of the Empire with respect to the priesthood.

Chapter VI

SOME ASPECTS OF THOUGHT
IN THE FOURTEENTH AND
FIFTEENTH CENTURIES

Since it is impossible, in a final chapter, to present an adequate picture of the intellectual life of the fourteenth and fifteenth centuries, still so filled with unknowns, we will confine our attention to only a few aspects. Leaving aside "the return of belles lettres" (Petrarch was a contemporary of Ockham), the continuity of Averroism, as well as other matters of culture or currents of thought, one can isolate several problems: speculative mysticism, criticism and speculation in metaphysics and theology, the philosophy or science of nature, and the analysis of the conditions of salvation.

Even before William of Ockham taught, Meister Eckhart had written and preached.[1] Books abound on this

[1] Eckhart, born about 1260 in Hochheim, near Gotha, was perhaps a student of Albert the Great in Cologne. He studied and

Saxon Dominican, who was accused of heresy in 1326 before the archbishop of Cologne, and twenty-six of whose propositions were, after his death, condemned by Pope John XXII. Some have defended his thought, if not his expression of it, from the viewpoint of the Church; others have maintained that he was an independent intellectual. In the present state of the publication and understanding of the texts, it seems difficult to recover the original sense of these theses in terms of their theological milieu. This would be an ultimate task, after a thorough study. This study remains to be done, but when it is said that Eckhart was a mystic, an explanation of the nature of this mysticism must be given. Richard of Saint-Victor and St. Bonaventure have taught us not to believe too readily that mysticism is opposed to scholasticism. What does the latter term mean to us? In the sense of a formation of the mind, a mental regimen, our Dominican was a scholastic, as the conception of his *Opus tripartitum* proves.

This work, in large part lost, was composed of three sections: an *Opus propositionum,* in which, in fourteen treatises, the author upheld more than a thousand theses —*propositiones tenet mille et amplius;* an *Opus quaestionum,* where questions were discussed in the same order as in the *Summa* of Thomas Aquinas; and an *Opus expositionum,* an exposition of Scripture, treated as a source for authorities. The *Opus propositionum* dominates the other two. There is, for example, beside the first proposition ("Being is God"—*Esse est Deus*), a first question ("Does God exist?"—*Utrum Deus sit*) and a first authority ("In the beginning, God created heaven and earth"—*In principio creavit Deus caelum et terram*). The truth of the proposition is demonstrated; from it, the answer to

---

taught at Paris in 1300-02, was the Dominican provincial for Saxony from 1303 to 1317; he preached with great success, especially in Strasbourg, and taught at Cologne, where in 1326 he was cited before the archbishop's tribunal; he appealed to the pope on February 13, 1327, probably the year of his death. The condemnation of John XXII followed on March 27, 1329.

the question is derived—*ex propositione jam declarata*
("from the proposition already expounded")—and the
cited authority is explained—*ex praemissa propositione*
("from the previously established proposition"). Such is
the method presented by the master, who adds: "Beginning with this first proposition, by reasoning well, all or
almost all questions relative to God are resolved, and by
natural reason most texts which speak of Him are clearly
explained, even those that are obscure and difficult." His
purpose then is to answer questions and to interpret texts.
With dialectic and exegesis (biblical commentaries occupy
an important place in Eckhart's work), we encounter
again the medieval surroundings of *doctrina sacra*.

Without prejudicing the significance of his Latin scholastic works, it is convenient to indicate here the existence
of other treatises in German that have merited for their
author titles such as "the creator of German prose" and
"the father of German speculation." These judgments on
the influence of the master are of no concern for our
purpose. Let us simply take, as a point of departure for
a few remarks, the earliest Latin writings in which one
scholar, G. della Volpe, has found "the primitive and
essential core" of his mysticism, the basis that he establishes for union with God: in a doctrine apparently opposed to the first proposition of the *Opus tripartitum* on
the identity of Being and God.

During the school year of 1302-03, Eckhart was teaching at Paris as a master in theology; he had a dispute with
another master, the Franciscan Gonsalvus of Balboa, on
the sidelines of which Duns Scotus, then a "Bachelor
Sententiary," can be discerned. Let us examine the question in these circumstances: *Utrum in Deo sit idem esse
et intelligere*—"Whether in God to *be* and to *know* is
the same thing?" Knowing through the intellect is meant,
and the question depends on another about intellection
in angels. The German Dominican does indeed posit the
identity in God of being with intellection, as well as with
every other action: "being is knowing . . . through being

[God] does all things"—*ipsum esse est ipsum intelligere . . . per ipsum esse omnia operatur*. But to this identification he also gives the sense of a certain primacy of intellect over being: "Because He knows, by that He is . . . it is the knowing itself that is the foundation of being itself"—*quia intelligit ideo est . . . est ipsum intelligere fundamentum ipsius esse*. There is a transcendence of knowledge: "To know is higher than to be"—*intelligere est altius quam esse*. Being in fact is what Aristotle divides into his ten categories, the definite, the determined in genera and species; knowing, on the contrary, seems in itself to be characterized by indetermination, by infinity: "There is something indeterminate about the intellect and knowing . . . an action of this kind [to know through the intellect] is purely infinite"—*intellectus et intelligere est aliquid indeterminatum . . . talis actio [sc. intelligere] est infinita simpliciter*. Our two questions refer— once again!—to Aristotle's *De anima:* an intellect that must extend to all ought not to be mingled with anything in particular, restrained by a nature. This "illimitation" of the intelligence in act indicates here the transcendence of God, His purity (*puritas essendi*) as opposed to being that is defined by determination, as caused or "creatable." By juxtaposing "being," conceived in this way, and "pure knowing," the created is distinguished from the uncreated. A Latin sermon later annotated by Nicholas of Cusa teaches that if in intellectual beings without matter, the divine unity is not found (*sunt non unum*), this is because their essence is not their being (*esse*); or rather that their being is not to know (*quia ipsorum esse non est intelligere*) in the absolute sense that this last term has for Eckhart. Although to maintain being in the order of the created, the *Quaestiones Parisienses* cite the *De causis*, they refer to the Bible to exalt knowledge, invoking the primacy of the Word, completely turned toward the intellect which speaks to it (*se toto est ad intellectum, et est ibi dicens et dictum*), and invoking also a perennial theme, the uncreated character of Wisdom. Nor does the Parisian master allow himself to oppose the famous text of Exodus which for Thomas Aquinas and Duns Scotus justified their use of being (although differently conceived in other respects) in theology. Anticipating a modern exegesis, Eckhart maintains that by saying: *Ego sum qui sum,* God does not reveal His name, but rather refuses to state His name.

In the course of his career, by elevating being to the point of identifying it with God—*esse est Deus*—Eckhart did not renounce his exalted conception of knowing. When he saw it attacked, he defended the following thesis at the end of his life: *Una virtus est in anima, si anima esset tota talis, tunc esset increata*—"There is a force in the soul, the intellect, such that if the soul were completely composed of this, it would be uncreated." God, Meister Eckhart explains, has created man in His image, "so that he is intellect, like God himself, who is pure uncreated intellect, having nothing in common with anyone." Let us distinguish two ideas linked together here: *the uncreated, divinity,* and *pure intellect* are equivalent expressions; we are not purely intellect, but our intellect is the image of God, the temple, where He dwells in us. The connection of the two ideas is the result of the absolute character, of the purity of the knowing under discussion—a notion capable of manifesting both the transcendence of God and the possibility of union with him. As Nicholas of Cusa will note in the margin of the sermon already cited, if in God there is nothing of being other than knowing, it is only in the intellect that it will be possible to find "God as God." A person is united with Him by ascending in intellectuality—*ascendere ad intellectum.* In the mystic sense of the term *to know,* "we cannot know God unless we are God in some manner" (V. Delbos): such is, for Eckhart, the power of the intellect whose excellence he established against Gonsalvus of Balboa at the beginning of his career.

This Franciscan wanted the act of loving, not the act of knowing, to make man *deiform* (perfect in resemblance

to God)—*diligere est major deiformatio quam intelligere.*
As a reason why the soul is pleasing to God, Eckhart had
proposed the act of knowing: "One is pleasing to God
precisely because of knowing"—*aliquis praecise est Deo
gratus quia sciens.* Astonished, Gonsalvus wonders what
becomes of the value of charity when we abandon a
voluntarism according to which we rejoin God by the
faculty of loving, which is superior to that of knowing?
The Dominican master will however remain faithful to
his *intellectualism,* placing grace only in the intellect (*in
solo intellectu*), the seat of the divine image and of
mystical union. The latter will then be seen as "an extension of knowledge" or rather as knowledge itself, attaining its purity, its unity in God—the God, that is, of
Israel who, according to our Latin sermon, is the seeing
God and the God of those who see: *Deus Israel Deus
videns Deus videntium.* The principle of union, comprehensible only by the intellect (*solo intellectu capitur*),
wholly intellect, the cause of unity, He is the one God—
qui est intellectus se toto Deus unus est. By remarking
that to call Him one and to call Him wholly intellect are
in this case "one and the same thing," Gilson perhaps
suggests how to surmount a difficulty encountered at the
highest level of the doctrine or rather of the experience
of the mystical theologian.

The abode of the saved, identical with the ultimate
principle, eternal movement in a Unity of indistinction
and repose, is apparently located beyond the Trinity and
its processions. Already noted in speaking of Erigena, this
difficulty is encountered not only by Christian mystics
influenced by the Neoplatonic One; it reappears in the
speculation of Duns Scotus. His metaphysics allows him
to conceive of a distinction between the divine essence
and the constitutive properties of the persons such that
it is necessary to envision this essence apart from the
persons, as a possible object of intuition and beatifying
love. Although in fact, in the order of salvation freely
established by God, the essence is not given without

the persons, it remains absolutely possible—*de potentia Dei absoluta*—that it can be. In a very different context, apart from the Trinity, outside relationships, and inter-personal life, does not the mysticism of Eckhart, who is also a dialectician, offer the solitude and "the desert" of the Deity—the essence which, according to the tradi-tional formula, "does not engender," distinct from the Father who is, by His very paternity, "fecundity, germina-tion, production"? This distinction, says a text, is imposed "according to our mode of knowing." But is this a question of knowledge by concepts exterior to the real, where the one can be separated from the other? The impossibility of distinguishing two objects is perhaps made evident by the dialectical identification Gilson notes: "Unity is pater-nity"—a comprehensible identification if this is a case of the unity of an intellect involving a Word, in the identity of a reflection about itself. In approaching a point of view in which essence and Father seem insepa-rable, one should sense the co-existence, emphasized by Rudolf Otto, of the two aspects of the divine according to the Thuringian master—cessation and repose, on the one hand, and on the other, flux, "boiling," vitality.

This mysticism in which a Word incarnate can lead to his Father and to the Deity in him, presupposes the notion of a knowing or an understanding (*intelligere*) who is God; it does not exclude the possibility that being (*esse*) is equally God, provided that this term has a meaning other than that adopted in the *Quaestiones Parisienses*. In the *Opus propositionum*, this new sense is found in a very simple dialectic, which depends on the idea of Creation: if all things are through being, as all white objects are white through whiteness—*sicut omnia sunt alba ab albedine*—it is necessary that, to remain the Creator, God must be *the* being—*omne, quod est, per esse est. Esse autem Deus est.* Identical with God, es-pecially the Holy Spirit, *the* being who, comparable to whiteness, acts as a form, holds the same place in the world as the soul does in the body—the soul being conceived in the manner of Albert the Great (B. J. Muller-Thym). Divine, therefore unique, this *esse* does not immediately make such and such a creature exist, but rather all of Creation: the universe that the first cause has in mind from the beginning, before its parts—*totum universum est primo intentum a causa prima.* Since the unity of the created world corresponds to that of the Creator, Eckhart sees one question "perish," Avicenna's difficulty which still "weighs" on his contemporaries: How can the multiplicity of beings be immediately derived from the unique Principle? Perhaps even more than its cosmic aspect, the religious sense of this ontology must be noted. Following Rudolf Otto, Gilson too evokes the Lutheran doctrine of justification: *the* being, he says, is here "imputed to beings by God without ever becoming their own being," always in the act of being created, like the just of Luther, always on the way to be justified, by an imputed, never by a "proper," justice. Eckhart also writes: *Justus ut sic totum suum esse accipit ab ipsa justitia*—the just man as such receives all that he is from *the* justice itself, who is God, the transcendent term for the analogy by which this perfection is attributed to a creature. But must one also hold, with Rudolf Otto, that his speculative mysticism is "colored" or rather "permeated" with the Christian doctrine of justification?

As Gilson notes, Johannes Tauler, Heinrich Suso, and John Ruysbroeck, the "masters of Christian spirituality," are Eckhart's continuers. The work of the first will exercise an influence on Luther, who will edit a treatise, the *Theologica Germanica,* issuing from this spiritual milieu. Tauler notes in one of his sermons, with respect to the doctrine of a "recess" or a "point" of the mind—*abditum . . . apex mentis*—, the continuity of thought from Albert the Great to Dietrich of Freiberg and Meister Eckhart. Ruysbroeck's *Adornment of Spiritual Nuptials* was sharply criticized by John Gerson who, by utilizing nominalism intended to rescue mystical theology, which he extolled, from perilous speculative implications and

to make it an instrument of spiritual and university reform. He was concerned with wresting theologians from
this vain curiosity in matters of faith which enticed even
Franciscans like the Scotist John of Ripa to analyze and
subdivide the essence of God by means of "formal distinctions." On the other hand, it was the speculative
fecundity of the mystical writings that drew Cardinal
Nicholas of Cusa[2] to Eckhart, as well as to Erigena and
Proclus: a great savant and humanist, Nicholas continues
the tradition of the Pseudo-Denis and the medieval elaboration of the idea of the infinite. In order to consider
the infinite as infinite (*infinitum ut infinitum*), one must
know it as unknown (*ignotum*), in the manner of the
mystics' "vision of the invisible God." By making op-
posites coincide (maximum and minimum, necessary and
impossible), the method of "learned ignorance" contradicts Aristotelian logic from which Nicholas, in the middle
of the fifteenth century, says his contemporaries cannot
detach themselves without a veritable conversion. In this
doctrine of an Absolute involving everything, even contradictions, of an intellect in opposition to discursive reason, Aristotle is deliberately abandoned, but Christ
remains, with grace and faith—the subject, after God
and the world, of the third and last book of the *De docta
ignorantia.*

Nicolas d'Autrecourt, a Parisian master condemned in
1346, is a good example, an extreme case, of the kind of
criticism that has held the attention of historians of
philosophy, while we remain ignorant of many other
doctrines of the same period. In Aristotle and his commentator Averroës, Nicolas finds a multitude of theses.
Have they really been *demonstrated,* that is to say, did
the Philosopher really *know* them? Such being the question, he had to answer in the negative; the principal

[2] Johannes Tauler: 1300-61, Heinrich Suso: 1300-65, John Ruysbroeck: 1293-1381, John Gerson: 1363-1429, Nicholas of Cusa:
1401-64.

doctrines of Peripateticism do not admit of demonstration, they do not constitute knowledge. This conclusion is enunciated in a defiant tone and with a triumphant accent. We are in the midst of a controversy.

Let us reason in a rigorously logical way. Let us recall William of Ockham: all of our knowledge is analyzed into propositions, guided by the principle of noncontradiction. Logical evidence is confounded with identity, it is reduced to the first principle. In a mind that knows only evidence reduced in this way—*evidentia reducta in primum principium*—reasoning would not know how to construct anything. Purely analytical, discourse brings about the creation of nothing new: "everything apparent as a result of discourse is apparent before such discourse" —*quaecumque est res apparens esse consequenter discursui est apparens ante discursum.* Everything that we posit must be given us before reasoning. Four centuries later, Kant will remark that a strictly logical judgment cannot link one existence to another; the attitude of Nicolas d'Autrecourt is not so different: "From the fact that one thing is known to *be,* it cannot be inferred as evident that something else *may be*"—*Ex eo quod aliqua res est cognita esse, non potest evidenter inferri quod alia res sit.* If there is no possibility of inference from one similar thing to another, it would neither be possible to draw conclusions about a substance from sensible appearances nor to hold that the causal bond is necessary: accident and substance, cause and effect, are not linked together in a proof under pain of contradiction. There is the same lack of evidence for finality and for the necessity of positing degrees of perfection among things. Nicolas finds that it is impossible to logically establish any of the fundamental Aristotelian concepts. This fourteenth-century criticism even reached what, in the eyes of historians, constitutes the central intuition of the natural philosophy of Aristotle: the idea of a real change, by which substances pass from non-being into being or, inversely, from "generation" to "corruption." On the contrary, one of

Nicolas's theses affirms that "it cannot be clearly shown that all things are not eternal," ungenerated, incorruptible —*non potest evidenter ostendi, quin quaelibet res sit aeterna.* Can it be truly *known* that certain things, sensible qualities for example, are not eternal? One color gives way to another; the knowledge of this alteration is analyzed in terms of contradictory propositions—the affirmation of the first color; the negation of this same color. We remain in a thought where all certitude is expressed in logical form, including the perception of change. This constitutes a formidable method of criticism. At a given moment we cease to see an object, the color; we conclude that it no longer exists. This inference does not need to be accepted. It would be possible to suppose, in fact, that instead of becoming corrupt, natural forms are subdivided into parts so small that they escape apprehension by our senses: in such an atomistic perspective there would be eternal things. This then is the experiment that Master Nicolas performs on Peripateticism: he begins with a completely logical notion of evidence, which his adversary, if he is in the spirit of the times, seemingly cannot refuse; he then asserts the impossibility of having any certitude about the existence of material substances, causes, ends, degrees of perfection, generation and corruption.

We have asked the Philosopher for his evidence; we have found only lack of evidence. Incapable of demonstrating the essentials of their doctrine, his disciples do not *know* what they teach. A word which constantly recurs characterizes this test: *evidenter.* A second experiment, also on Aristotle, is formulated from another point of view, which is embodied in the term *probabile,* or rather in the expression: *conclusio probabilior conclusione opposita* ("a thesis more probable than the opposing thesis"). Nicolas moves from one point of view to the other, discussing the question of the eternity of things and its opposite, the possibility of the corruption or fall of being into non-being. We have shown that the Aristotelians have no certainty about corruption; can we, on the other hand, have any certainty about eternity, conceived in the same way? Nicolas d'Autrecourt thinks not: he asserts that being corruptible is repugnant and implies a contradiction—*esse corruptibile includit repugnantiam et contradictionem*. But this contradiction does not appear in terms that constitute the subject of a proposition, and the proposition is not proven by a simple analysis of concepts—*per explicationem conceptuum*. To prove this, our enemy of Aristotle does not question the simple notion of being corruptible, he involves it in an idea of the universe; it is impossible, he explains, to say that "a being constituting a part of an always equally perfect ensemble is corruptible"—*ens pars totius semper aequaliter perfecti, corruptibile*. What is the source of this conception of a Whole whose constantly equal perfection would prevent the passing away of any of its parts? Due to the demands of finality or a principle of the better, the good seems to be the only explicable disposition of things; for there is an infinity of others, of evils; the bad is something indeterminate. If the good is abandoned for its negation, it is impossible to find a greater reason for such a manner of being than for some other, and so on to infinity. Since the bad, or the negation of the good, is an infinity, if it were realized in a certain disposition, it could be, for the same reason, realized in another disposition or in an infinity of ways—*Quia malum sive negatio boni est infinita, et ideo, qua ratione fieret secundum unam dispositionem, eudem ratione secundum aliam vel modis infinitis*. The formula is worthy of Leibnitz. To this principle, Nicolas joins three others: the idea of the mutual connection of all beings; the idea that nothing exists except for the good of the whole; and finally, the idea that the universe is always equal to itself in perfection. In this perspective, nothing real exists in vain, nothing could disappear without disorder; the corruption of a being is inconceivable; the eternity of each is therefore necessary. The argument is developed with full consciousness of its principles of finality and the better: "It was necessary for me," says Nicolas, "to have recourse to the final cause and to show that it is better to say that things are eternal"—*Oportuit me recurrere ad causam finalem et ostendere quod melius est dicere res aeternas.* The thesis of the eternity of things seems to be more valid than its opposite: *Magis est assentiendum quam oppositae* ("It is better to assent to this than to the opposite"). That no being perishes is not posited as a thesis. Rather it is proposed as the most probable hypothesis.

What is constantly questioned is the reality of a substantial alteration, the rhythm of Aristotelian nature passing from birth to death: *corruptio unius, generatio alterius.* The refutation is accomplished in two steps: Aristotle, on the one hand, did not know how to demonstrate his thesis; and on the other, in the very order of proofs that do not constitute demonstrations, his adversary sweeps him away. Nicolas d'Autrecourt offers us a remarkable understanding of this order of the *probabile:* two opposing theses are put in the presence of one another; each asserts its reasons; the discussion is the decisive test; as for the judge, he is wholeheartedly in love with the truth, without partiality in the matter; it is his task to appraise the degree of probability of both opinions, and to decide on which side he finds an excess —*gradus probabilitatis excedens.* This conception of probability is the consequence of the arguments that have been furnished: after Nicolas has formulated his arguments, his contemporaries can no longer acknowledge the traditional validity of the ideas of generation and corruption. Their probability is at present found to be reduced to the advantage of the opposing idea; but in the future, some other dialectician may be able to reverse this advantage. The *probabile* constitutes a momentary, transitory value; there is nothing definitive about it. This is why, of the two theses, the more probable is not necessarily the true one, and however forceful they may be, probabilities never enter into competition with the certainties of faith. After having shown how, in the atomism he proposes, the just will be rewarded and the wicked punished, Nicolas d'Autrecourt can remark that this hypothesis, the most likely in the present state of understanding, will perhaps one day loose its validity. "Let us adhere," he concludes, "to the law of Christ and believe that the recompense of the good and the punishment of the bad will never take place in any other way than is stated in this sacred law." Elsewhere he says: "That all things are not eternal, is true; I know it, and the Catholic faith affirms it; and I do not believe what contradicts this. I only say that according to the natural appearances in which we presently participate, the eternity of beings is more probable than the opposite thesis."

In effect, then, the only concern is to show the vanity of Aristotelian metaphysics and natural philosophy from the Aristotelian point of view, which is both scientific and dialectic. In the light of his first principle, it is established that Aristotle does not *know* what he affirms; by using philosophical concepts such as finality, it is possible to demonstrate the improbability of such a central conception, basic to the Peripatetic philosophy of nature, while holding at the same time with the Philosopher that the true does not necessarily coincide with the most probable. Nicolas was able to present his discussions as school exercises, knowing at the same time that these exercises departed from the scholastic university tradition. Nicolas questions an entire mental regimen: having considered "the doctrine of Aristotle and of his commentator Averroës and the thousand theses they affirm," when with equal probability it is possible to maintain the opposite, this master of arts sees his contemporaries "pass twenty or thirty years of their life in the study of this doctrine, until the age of decrepitude." Let us cite another passage from the astonishing prologue of his treatise *Exigit ordo executionis:* "I considered the manner in which, for the sake of the logical terms of Aristotle and Averroës, all these men abandoned questions of morality and the care of the common good." Nicolas was himself a logician, but one who utilized the instrument of logic to prove the inanity of scholasticism. Yielding to a kind of prophetic inspiration, he perceives in the future "some divine men who will no longer consume the whole of their lives in logical discourses or in the analysis of obscure Aristotelian propositions, but who will communicate to the people an understanding of divine law." Once the small degree of certitude derived from natural philosophy and from metaphysics, which is its continuation, has been asserted, how is it possible to avoid turning one's attention to morality? This criticism of the speculative tradition seeks to make men adhere solely to the law of Christ. Our hero is not surprised at the opposition he stirs up: does he not play the role of the friend of truth who has arisen, among sleeping men, sounding his trumpet to rouse them from their sleep?—*Cum insurrexit amicus veritatis et suam fecit sonare tubam ut dormientes a somno excitaret?* Here already, it has been said, in the middle of the fourteenth century, is the sound of the Renaissance, or of the Reformation. If, for the Middle Ages, Aristotle represents not only jointly or separately liable theses but a mode of thought converted into the scholastic tradition, it is a whole culture that seems essentially vain to Nicolas d'Autrecourt.

Even if other symptoms of crisis can be found in his age, his thought preserves an extreme character that tends to isolate it. It has often been admitted that it merely deduces the consequences of the principles posed by Ockham, but there are, in the philosophy of knowledge, positions of Ockham held by Nicolas's adversaries. Nicolas's method of admitting as evidence only what can be reduced to the principle of identity was denounced by

his contemporary, Jean Buridan,[3] an important repre-
sentative of "terminism," that is to say nominalism.
Buridan refuses to allow the physical and moral sciences
—*scientiae naturales et morales*—to be ruined under the
pretext that their truths are not imposed under pain of
contradiction and do not restrict the power of God, who
is always capable of freeing Himself from the natural
order which He has freely instituted. Granted such an
order—*ex suppositione naturae*—there exists a zone of
relative evidence—*evidentia ex suppositione*—much
greater in extent than that of absolute evidence—*evidentia simplex* (E. A. Moody). This "moderate" attitude
is also found in another Parisian master, Cardinal Pierre
d'Ailly. This nominalist does not overestimate the value
of Aristotelian proofs. On that of the first cause, he remarks: "From this argument it can be seen that there are
few if any clearly demonstrable proofs in the philosophy
or doctrine of Aristotle. In reality, this proof seems the
most obvious of all those that Aristotle had ever formulated. Let us conclude then that the philosophy or doctrine
of Aristotle deserves the name of opinion rather than of
knowledge. Consequently, those people who obstinately
adhere to the authority of Aristotle are most reprehen-
sible." Our theologian nevertheless takes up the classical
argument and endeavors to give it the highest probability.

We are not then in an intellectual world which requires
absolute evidence in every instance. Here thought subsists on that probability Descartes will attempt to exclude
from the speculative order. "In truth," says Pierre d'Ailly,
"it is not at all necessary that an evidence be of the
highest order, for evidence admits of different degrees"—
*De facto non est necesse evidentiam de aliquo esse sum-
mam, immo in evidentia sunt gradus.* Alongside uncondi-

[3] Jean Buridan, born in Bethune, rector of the University of
Paris in 1328 and 1340, still active in 1358, has left the work
of a master in arts. Pierre d'Ailly, 1350-1420, read the *Sentences*
in 1375.

tional evidence, which coincides with that of the principle of noncontradiction, Ailly admits a conditional evidence —*evidentia conditionata*—which is valid only within the hypothesis of a natural order established and respected by God, being given his general [and not special] influence and the customary course of nature and the absence of the miraculous—*stante Dei influentia generali et cursu naturae solito nulloque facto miraculo*. Admitting only a natural order, an order of certitudes is imposed; it comprises all knowledge derived from the positing of second causes, of natures endowed with efficacy. In our study of Ockham, we noted that God was able to do anything by his own power; it will never be *demonstrated* that any other being can truly act. Thus, as both the celebrated Franciscan and our cardinal admit, we are not rigorously assured of the existence of objects, the causes of our perception; in a miraculous fashion, the Creator can cause an impression in our senses, without the aid of any creature. To avoid this kind of doubt in any particular question, it is both necessary and sufficient that the absence of the miraculous be agreed upon. The same thing is true for each case of causality. This does not mean that Pierre d'Ailly or Ockham denies the reality of second causes, endowed with efficacy: they merely posit that, subordinated to the Almighty of the Bible, Aristotelian nature is never absolutely assured of exerting its proper force. Would it not then be absurd to require a certainty superior to the *probabile* in matters essentially dependent on divine liberty? These theologians do not, as some have thought, criticize the very idea of causality; with complete confidence they apply it to matters that fit Aristotelian situations. They do not envision the replacement of an obscure efficacy by simple constancies, but they color the certitude of secondary causality with a theological reservation about the principle. The conception of things does not change so much; only its degree of evidence is made more precise. This example of efficacious causes shows us minds at rest in the "probable," the sense of which must, it seems, be made precise in each case. It would be possible to cite other examples of terminist moderation: Jean Buridan and his disciple Marsilius of Inghen[4] both indicate that it is not necessary to require the same rigor in proof from the metaphysician as from the mathematician.

When, as we have indicated in the preceding chapter, Ockhamists still sought a certain understanding of faith, speculative ardor and originality did not abandon all of their contemporaries who followed other schools of thought and who had received a different training. Thus the Franciscan disciples of Scotus were not uncritical of their master. This intellectual independence is apparent in François de Meyronnes and John of Ripa[5] who will serve to illustrate two significant examples of Scotist speculation in the fourteenth century—a doctrine of being as perfection, and a doctrine of divine essence as the "form" of a saved soul.

In the first question of his commentary on the *Sentences* (in the definitive edition), François de Meyronnes, known in the schools as the "Prince of the Scotists," asks if the first principle—of identity or noncontradiction—formulated by Aristotle is valid in theology; his answer is affirmative, the logical difficulties caused by the Trinity being the result of the formal distinction of multiple "formalities" in the midst of the same absolutely indivisible reality—*plures formalitates in eadem re penitus indivisa*. Concerning the univocal being of Scotus, the first in a formal ontology, the universally valid discipline, François de Meyronnes holds that this first metaphysical principle is not imposed on objects, but found in them—*invenitur*. As independent of the existence of things as a

[4] Marsilius of Inghen, the rector of the University of Heidelberg, died in 1396.
[5] François de Meyronnes died in 1325. The *Determinationes* of John of Ripa date from 1358 or 1359; we are indebted for our knowledge of the texts to A. Combes, who is preparing an edition of them.

mental act, its objectivity, equivalent we could say to that of a "proposition in itself," recalls the "separation" of the Platonic Ideas—*videtur quoddam ens separatum*—which, distinguishing it from the caricature that Aristotle made of it, François attributes to the Scotist "essences" which must now be called on in order to comprehend the "formalities." By "formalizing" however, one is not lost in the unreal, but remains in the order of the possible whose nature it is to pass into existence—*natum moveri in rerum natura*. Being in itself—*ens simpliciter*—which is not just a fragment of something existing, is seen in this framework as a pure essence. In *our* knowledge, this "formal reason," the subject of the first principle, the object of first philosophy, has primacy over all others. The "our" must be underlined. For another "quidditative reason," the divinity or "deity" is absolutely first, even before being itself—*deitas est omnino prior ente*. The distinction and the relationship between metaphysics and theology is based on these two "formalities." In this plan, the divine nature must, in effect, be envisioned by itself, apart from the persons; to treat it in "reality," would be to substitute a "quaternity" for the Trinity: in this way François de Meyronnes avoids the danger which, according to Pierre d'Auriol, menaces the Trinitarian theology of Scotus.

The absolute primacy and the radical simplicity of the deity prohibit including it in *the* being, conceiving of it as a "part" of this "quiddity." Given this distinction between God as God and "the being that is only being," it will no doubt be asked: How *is* God being? François answers by saying that, with respect to their formal distinction, the infinity of all perfections identifies them one with another, but being is a pure perfection—*perfectio simpliciter*—which, communicated by Creation, is found in a finite degree in the created and, when restored in thought to an infinite degree, permits us to conceive of the Creator. Like all communicable perfections, common both to the created and the uncreated, *the* being belongs to the sphere of natural knowledge, while the deity, since it is incommunicable outside the circle of divine persons, remains naturally unknowable to every created spirit: "the source of all perfections" in the mystery which Denis has described according to the experience of St. Paul. When envisioned in this way in its "ultimate precision," the divine essence occupies a position beyond being, beyond infinity itself, which is one of its modes; when placed in the grandeur or the intensity of being, infinity is the mode by which it finds it possesses all perfections (that is, communicable perfections, like being or, rather, "entity") through an identity excluding all progressive determination, all potential indetermination. This dialectic of the other and the same, a logic of the infinite, establishes an equilibrium in the analysis of the "formalities" which does not destroy the unity of God.

The technique of John of Ripa, more difficult and complex than that of François de Meyronnes, entitles him to represent in Gerson's eyes the virtuosi of the formal distinction (*formalizantes*), who utilized it more frequently and with greater profundity than Scotus. Leaving aside the destiny of this distinction in the second half of the fourteenth century, as well as the paradoxical and even condemned theses that it inspired, let us consider instead the method of a "prolix but astonishingly vigorous theologian" (A. Combes), who formulates in his "metaphysical algebra" the problems of the union of the soul with God in beatitude and correlatively in justification or rather sanctification—*in sanctificatione et in beatitudine*. The theological tradition that links these questions to that of the knowledge of Christ, previously indicated with respect to St. Bonaventure, has kept the name of John of Ripa by attributing to him, concerning the vision of God, a doctrine that he rejected "with more energy than precision." If he gives the divine essence the role of a "form" in the knowledge (*formalis notitia*) that a soul can have of it, it is by discarding a so-called "information" or communication from the very being of God—*informatio et communicatio divini esse*. Let us note what seems to have defined salvation for certain of his contemporaries (*moderni*) who invoked in this regard the Christology of Hugh of Saint-Victor. If being the object of knowledge (*notitia objectiva*) does not completely describe the function of the infinite essence in beatitude, this is because this immeasurable God (*Deus immensus*) immediately present in Himself to the faculty of knowing, perfects it through modification by a vital action (*vitalis immutatio*). Since it is absolutely inaccessible to every created spirit, the notion of a natural beatitude is excluded; the divine essence acts like a grace, an immeasurable light (*lux immensa*), through which the creature is infinitely and supernaturally lifted above itself—*infinita supra se supernaturaliter elevatur*. Here the object of knowledge is not assigned to the horizon of knowing simply in order to "define" it—*notitia objectiva praecise terminativa*. It is united with the faculty of the understanding spreading out in it—*unio intentionalis*—a union of the same kind that Peter Lombard, following St. Augustine, recognized between our will and the Holy Spirit, Uncreated Grace, in the sanctification or justification that makes us "pleasing to God" (*gratificatio*). To this doctrine of the Master of the Sentences, which we will encounter again at the end of this chapter, John of Ripa applies his ability for technical elaboration.

Whether it is a question of the divine vision or the state of grace, the essential thing is to distinguish the two kinds of relationships which exist between a form and that of which it is the form—*percipere distinctionem de habitudine informationis et vitalis immutationis*. In both his commentary on the *Sentences* and his *Determinationes*, our Franciscan confronts his adversaries by arming himself with this distinction. If he assigns a "formal" role to the uncreated, with respect to the created, it is only after having elaborated the concept of form in its relationship, first of all with matter, then with a vital act, such as perception or vision; and having linked it with an action, he does not imply that there is a relationship of "informing"—that is, of inherence and composition—with that on which it acts. As in the natural philosophers of the period, the forms act here by degrees and infinite degrees, according to their intensity. One can guess what interest was aroused by these philosophical analyses of a Prologue "to unusual propositions" which formed an introduction to theological knowledge by the analysis of its highest degree, the constitution of beatitude. "The philosophers" who have, in their own way and not without errors, dealt with the latter as the union (*copulatio*) of an active intellect identified with God and the possible intellect of Averroës, are called upon here. To a systematic exposition of the Peripatetic doctrine of intellects which belongs to the tradition (as B. Nardi has shown) linking Siger de Brabant with the Italian Averroists of the Renaissance, John of Ripa adds an interpretation of Platonism that leads likewise to a concept of formal union (*copulatio formalis*) of the soul with God. This utilization of so much erudition and skill indicates the great interest of fourteenth-century scholasticism in the problem and conditions of salvation—of beatitude in the future life and in its anticipation in the present Christian life through mystical union.

Pierre Duhem's work at the beginning of this century created a picture of the natural philosophy of the fourteenth century as a preparation for the science of the sixteenth and seventeenth centuries, especially in the speculation of the Parisian masters Jean Buridan, Albert of Saxony, and Nicole d'Oresme.[6] The works of Oresme would seem to permit one to think of Copernicus and the movement of the earth, of Galileo and the law of falling bodies, and of Descartes and analytical geometry. Since then, further studies—Galilean on the one hand, medieval (in particular the work of Anneliese Maier) on the other

[6] Albert of Saxony taught at Paris beginning in 1351; he became the first rector of the University of Vienna in 1365 and died in 1390. Nicole d'Oresme became a master in theology in 1362. He translated Aristotle's *Ethics* and *Politics* into French, wrote a treatise on money, and died in 1382.

—have minimized their position as "precursors of Galileo." One scholar has written that "for the history of scientific thought, the popular conception of the Renaissance is established as being fundamentally true" (Koyré). To do justice to the Middle Ages does not require the diminution of the following period.

One point to remember is the questioning of Aristotle as an authority in physics. A contemporary of Ockham, the Scotist John Marbres, writes in his *Commentary on the Eight Books of the Physics* that natural philosophy as Aristotle transmitted it to us is erroneous, and not well founded—*philosophia naturalis tradita ab Aristotele est erronea et insufficienter tradita*. And more precisely: "I say that Aristotle has badly and falsely expressed himself not only from the theologian's point of view, but even from the point of view of the natural philosopher and of philosophical truth, either because he did not have full knowledge of natural things, or because, having it, he affirmed the opposite." The historical difficulty is to determine precisely to what position the extension of this state of mind led men who normally worked on the basis of Aristotelian texts. The questioning, even the rejection of certain theses is not the same as the "mutation" of the "frames of understanding itself," which is apparently implied by the advent of the "classical physics" that prevailed from the sixteenth century until the scientific revolution of the twentieth century.

Some medieval men seem to have nearly removed the obstacle that Aristotle's qualitative approach constituted for a mathematical theory of the real. But neither Oresme's identification of qualities, intensively greater (*intensiones*) with figures (*configurationes*), nor the systems of "calculus" of the Oxonian scholars Thomas Bradwardine and Richard Swineshead [7] supplied that mathematical lan-

---

[7] Richard Swineshead was a fellow of Merton College in 1348 and the author of the *Calculationes*. Thomas Bradwardine, born before 1290 and also associated with Merton College, became the archbishop of Canterbury in 1349, the year of his death.

guage with which early modern science will question nature and obtain an answer. Moreover, the fourteenth-century scholastics "resorted only to an a priori calculation without having sought any contact with experience . . ." (A. Maier).

It is in this way that Bradwardine "calculates" the relationships (*proportiones*—one is tempted to say "functions") between the factors of movement as they are conceived in his age. These are not—not even "swiftness" —measurable quantities. The dynamics of the Parisian natural philosophers is however at variance with Aristotle; the central notion is that of the *impetus*, a force impressed on the moved by the mover. Even in antiquity, the act of throwing constituted a major difficulty for the commentators of the *Physics*. For a "violent" motion, which does not correspond to the nature of the moving object, would seem to require the continuous action of the mover. When the moving object has been separated from the mover, the motion ought to cease. But once hurled, a projectile continues in its path: Aristotle explains this by means of a reaction with the surrounding medium. The explanation in terms of an *impetus* left by the mover (*vis derelicta*) in the moving object helped lead natural philosophers, including even Galileo, to abandon Aristotelian physics; it left men, however, with "a conception entirely different" from that of classical mechanics in which (uniform) movement conserves itself by itself.

If inertia understood in this way does not have the force of a principle except for bodies situated in the infinite and isomorphic space of geometry, one must be attentive to the criticism of the Aristotelian notion of "place," as a characteristic of the cosmos: "A place for everything and everything in its place" (Koyré). Hence the interest of speculations that tend to realize apparently "imaginary" space beyond the limits of the Universe: "Devoid of bodies," says Bradwardine, "but not of God." Theology intervenes again; Newton, too, will have recourse to it. But the questioning of Aristotelianism has already shattered the image of the world in some places.

Besides speculative mysticism, the tension between criticism and speculation, and the development of natural philosophy, voluntarism would seem to be another predominate aspect of fourteenth- and fifteenth-century thought. This term, classical but in need of clarification, was applied to both man and God. We know it in its application to man—that is, in terms of the problem of beatitude, one asks by what power of the intellect or the will the soul enters into the possession of the absolute Good, into the enjoyment of the divine Trinity. A common notion was that the act or state of beatitude is found in the highest faculty—*frui est in potentia nobilissima.* For Franciscans like Scotus and Ockham, union with God is effected by an act of the will, the love that possesses and enjoys. We find once again the theme of the excellence of charity: one Scotist text cites the authority of St. Paul against Aristotle's formula exalting a purely intellectual contemplation; the authority of *our* philosopher as Christians—*philosophus noster, scilicet Paulus*—is opposed to that of the Philosopher. In this regard, William of Ockham did not in any sense separate himself from his predecessor, with whom we have so often seen him disagree. According to the same tradition and inspiration, the nominalists identified the grace of salvation with the virtue of charity: Scripture in fact, Gabriel Biel thinks, attributes the same properties and the same excellence to them indifferently. It is this voluntarism that Meister Eckhart always resisted.

Duns Scotus rejected the primacy of knowing over being even before Gonsalvus of Balboa. To know, he says, does not come first in God, but what is first and what bestows being, is being itself—*Intelligere non est primum in Deo, sed primum dans esse est ipsum ens.* By representing the source of being in this way, one does not depart from the definition that the God of Exodus gave of Himself. What is absolutely fundamental in the divine is essence as essence—*Primum omnino in divinis est essentia ut essentia.* Let us not imagine a will as the ultimate foundation of the real. The metaphysical landscape here is quite different: in one sense (excluding the "quaternity": François de Meyronnes will explain that, since essence alone is not real, emanation—*profluxus realis*—begins with the Father), Scotus supposes that the principle of the Trinity is communicable essence. In the order of emanations, the generation of the Word precedes the procession of the Spirit who is Love. Thus knowledge goes before and will follows behind: "The motion that is absolutely first, is the natural motion of the divine intellect on account of its object" [to know the divine essence]—*Omnino prima motio est naturalis motio intellectus divini a suo objecto.* Confronted with these texts on the primacy of both essence and the act of knowing, one may well ask where a "primacy of will," frequently mentioned in connection with Scotus and his school, can be found. There appears to be nothing of this kind as long as divine acts are related only to divinity itself. But with respect to the other objects of divine acts, the order is reversed; the will takes precedence not only in creating, but also in knowing. Actually, being merely possible, a creature does not constitute a fully determined object of thought: for Duns Scotus the contingency of the created is such that not only can it be or not be, but it can continue to be or not be (to comprehend this point of view it suffices to think of the acts of human liberty). The purely possible is ambiguous and indeterminate. How then can it be defined and resolved in the divine understanding? By the very decision to create it: the "decree," the "determination" of the will which leaves as contingent the very thing that it posits.

This is one of the masterful ideas of Scotus in his opposition to what we have called Arabic "necessitarianism": the freedom within the divine principle saves the contingency of the world which proceeds from it. (We cannot deal here with either the implications of this idea or its subsequent destiny in John of Ripa or Thomas Bradwardine.) There

is no need then to represent completely constituted possibilities in the divine understanding, such that the will
could only select and endow them with reality. Here the
creative act is not only a constitutive of things in themselves, but also of certain objects in absolute thought. This
is a good example of the "divine phenomenology" that we
have previously discussed: an initiative of the will is
found to be required in order that the contingent may appear to the intellect and constitute an object for it. To
will is an act of love. A love of this sort could not be directed toward its objects as if they were pre-existing
values. The goodness of creatures instead proceeds from
the creative act: "Everything except God is good because
it is willed by God"—*Omne aliud a Deo est bonum quia
a Deo volitum.* This primacy of the divine will with respect to all created good is what constitutes voluntarism.
This is a question of a love that owes nothing to its objects but gives them everything: "For in God, to love is
the cause of the goodness of the object; this is why there
is no duty to love"—*In Deo autem diligere est causa
bonitatis et ideo nullum ibi est debitum diligendi.* In
eternity there is a kind of invention of beings, from which
their value and temporal existence are derived. We can
see how fundamental what Bréhier has happily termed
"the unreserved affirmation of what might be called the
historical character of the Christian vision of the universe"
is for the thought of Duns Scotus—a universe constituted
even in its eternal idea by a free action. Since this action
consists in giving, Scotus conceives of God in terms of
liberality. According to whether they receive more or less,
a hierarchy of beings that are better or worse is formed,
and since even divine acts are related to their objects,
creating love "passes" from one being to another, beginning
with the highest, who is Christ, the incarnation of the
Word. In this important characteristic of Scotus's theology, we encounter once more the tendency to analyze
"the creative life": its principle is free, but ordered, liberality. The order of predestination, in which Christ is first,

makes it possible to understand, but without making it a necessity, the history of salvation and nature as its condition.

The interior order in the eternal will disappears in the thought of Ockham, the opponent of all attempts at "divine psychology." The rejection of distinctions in God prohibits any priority of essence over intellect, of intellect over will or vice versa. God is, at the same time, being, knowing, and love in an absolute simplicity. But, although these distinctions are abolished, the relationship between the creative will and the value of creatures remains the same. God owes nothing to anyone: "To no one is God in any way a debtor"—*Deus nulli debitor est quocumque modo.* All created goodness proceeds from his will: "By the very fact that he wills a thing, it is done well and justly"—*Eo ipso quod ipse vult, bene et juste factum est.* This is said with respect to the principle of economy, against those who would utilize it to govern divine action: the divinity gives without having to calculate. Voluntarism this time confronts us with a gratuitous act, defying any analysis, since it is identified with a radically simple essence. What Baruzi has written about Luther can be applied to Ockham: his God is "a gift, a gift in the form of Himself, an absolute gift."

What does He give us? By saving us He gives Himself, in particular his Spirit, the third person of the Trinity, who is no less divine than the other two. This doctrine is associated not only with the ardor of mystics like St. Bernard and Richard of Saint-Victor; it is found in the most abstract questions of the various commentaries on the *Sentences.* However speculative it may seem, theology remains the science of salvation; beatitude is the goal. The virtues—faith, hope, and charity—are the paths which lead there; if one of them is found to be identical with God, by that we are put in touch with our end: *per virtutes fruimur, non eis, nisi forte aliqua virtus sit Deus, ut caritas.* In these terms Peter Lombard taught that, as a means of access to beatitude, the virtues do not constitute the object that the blessed enjoy, unless one of them, charity, is God. According to the Master of the Sentences, the virtues of faith and hope are "qualities of the soul," something created; the virtue of charity on the other hand is something uncreated—the Spirit who, by tradition, is love. Before criticizing this thesis, Thomas Aquinas indicates the reason for it: *Et hoc dicebat Magister propter excellentiam caritatis* ("The Master said this because of the excellence of charity"). He was concerned with exalting the charity that saves us, indicating its transcendence for every creature, making it not only a gift of God, but God Himself, giving Himself to the soul.

In the thirteenth century, Aristotelianism introduced into this question a term unknown to Peter Lombard: in philosophical language a virtue—as a disposition to accomplish certain acts—is called a *habitus*. The virtues known to the philosophers are acquired by man—habits, as we would say; the Middle Ages would say *habitus acquis*. But man cannot give himself the faith and hope of the theologians; these God puts in the soul. This is the essential idea of the *habitus infus*.

When confronted with Distinction XVII of Book I of the *Sentences*, Peter Lombard's commentators ask themselves if charity can be distinguished, as the Master of the Sentences had done, from the other two theological virtues as not being such a *habitus* in the sense of a created form. On this point, Thomas Aquinas rejects Peter Lombard and adopts the position that charity is a created form. For Thomas thinks that if an act of loving were to proceed only from the divine Spirit, the human soul would find itself *moved* but would not itself be the source of the action. What would then become of spontaneity, a constitutive part of voluntary action, of the will as the source of merit? The character of the voluntary would be removed; the character of merit would be excluded—*sic etiam tolleretur ratio volontarii, et excluderetur ratio meriti*. Moreover, the action of a nature derives its perfection from the fact that it proceeds from within; let us not make the love of God, man's supreme act, more imperfect than natural actions—*esset actus iste imperfectior actibus naturalibus.* This idea of human-divine co-operation exemplifies Thomistic naturalism. Since we are—according to Scripture—incapable of saving ourselves by our natural forces, by our acquired virtues alone, we must have a divine force, an infused gift. If it is a *habitus,* when once received, we *have* it, it belongs to us; a created form, it enters into our composition and is united with our substance; the act that saves him emanates in a voluntary, meritorious fashion from the man thus divinely enriched and renovated. M.-D. Chenu has expressed this very well: from the Thomistic point of view, he says, "the charity of Peter Lombard was not *our* love of God in the full sense of a human possession"; a *habitus* is a "having."

We can perceive here the unity between theology and philosophy: the problem concerns the salvation of a nature, but it is not accomplished from without, by an extraneous grace. Nothing could be more in opposition to the subsequent spirit of the Lutheran reform. Harnack correctly saw the importance of this question; according to him, the great error of medieval theology was to have decided that we *merit* salvation, that the free will *co-operates* with grace, which in itself was likened to a virtue, the source of a value interior and proper *to us.* By their estrangement from Peter Lombard, the doctors of the thirteenth century opposed in advance the spirit of the Evangelical Church. These abstract doctrines touch the very foundation of religious life. During the fourteenth and fifteenth centuries as well, the thesis of the Master of the Sentences was generally rejected by the Schoolmen. Duns Scotus, Ockham, the nominalists all would no doubt agree that things *could* happen as Peter Lombard had said, since the *habitus* of charity constitutes one of those second causes for which, rigorously speaking, an omnipotent first cause has no need. But this possibility is not realized; to save ourselves, we receive this created gift, by an act of the liberality of God, as the result of one of those instances

of superabundance found in his work. Along with this
concept of "having" received, the ideas of voluntary spontaneity and of individual, meritorious works are found in
Scotist and Ockhamist doctrines. Within the order of
grace in which it is accomplished, human nature always
co-operates for its own salvation. William of Ockham,
Pierre d'Ailly, and Gabriel Biel consider created causality
as indemonstrable and hold it as *probabile*—in the eyes of
reason. But, among the data of faith, they put the notion
of merit, the idea of our efficacy: these theologians do
not find in Scripture what Luther had "to discover there,"
a Gospel of the servile will. The naturalism discussed with
respect to St. Thomas remains an essential theme for the
interpretation of the mentality of the later Middle Ages.

We already know of Duns Scotus's tendency to exalt
nature, further even than Thomism; this *dignificare naturam* was apparent to us in his conception of the intellect.
The same spirit can be observed in his idea of the will
with its emphasis on the freedom of the will. Here Ockham and Gabriel Biel continue Scotus; all of these theologians posit a *natural* capacity to love God above all
things. Within the limits of the present essay, we must
discuss this thesis by itself and without nuances—an abstraction made from the universal order which assigns to
it its exact sense, without considering the actual conditions which, in Biel, for example, reduce it in practice to
a borderline case. This basic position is the manifestation
of a state of mind, of a fundamental attitude. Gabriel Biel
reasons as follows: To love God above all things answers
to a commandment of right reason; to such a commandment, the will can conform by its natural forces. Such is
the coherence of our nature. If the will were merely
capable of being deficient with respect to reason, its action would necessarily be bad; it would naturally be bad
in itself—*alioquin esset naturaliter mala*. Biel, who has
been called "the last of the scholastics," remains faithful to
Ockham and Duns Scotus, despite Gregory of Rimini's
violent criticisms. With an astonishing and fierce rigor,

Gregory utilized a passage in St. Augustine according to which free will suffices for evil, but is of little use for good, unless it is aided by the omnipotent Good:—*liberum arbitrium ad malum sufficit, ad bonum autem parum est nisi adjuvetur ab omnipotente bono.* Every morally good act would require from God special assistance that is absent from an evil act or from purely physical actions; this thesis would hold even for Adam before the Fall. This has nothing to do with a consideration of reality, relative to our misery because of sin, but with an original state. "Let us abandon," says Gregory, "this thought that creatures can by themselves become better than the Creator made them." For Gabriel Biel, on the contrary, free will must—in principle—be able to accomplish good just as well as evil—*pari ratione;* a will capable only of failing seems to him evil by nature. There was no need to reason further; it seemed to him that his refutation of Gregory of Rimini had been definitively established: in every doctrine of the Creation, there is one nature, a gift of God, in which the good coincides with being itself. Does Genesis not say that on the evening after the Creation the Lord saw all the things that he had made, and that they were exceedingly good—*vidit Deus cuncta quae fecerat, et erant valde bona?* Naturalism, exalting free will in mankind, concurs with a basic optimism: the Fall of Adam can be overcome; since his sons are still men, a substantially good nature necessarily remains beneath their original sin. Let us agree with Gilson, that "the essential result" of medieval thought is the affirmation of the active, efficacious "intrinsic goodness" of nature, particularly in man.

A parallel idea of human value, founded in God, is apparent in the account we have given of Duns Scotus. Let us merely add another characteristic. Generally, philosophers of religion see in the fact of *being created* only a negative aspect, a lesson of deficiency—the discovery of our finiteness, of our quasi-nothingness in comparison with the Infinite. For the great Franciscan doctor, this idea of the making of a creature has a positive aspect for man, it carries a lesson of strength and dignity. Our intellectual nature proceeds from God who alone makes souls; such a being born by Creation could corrupt himself only through annihilation. A creature through his fault cannot in any way destroy, even in himself, the work of the Creator; this is why our sin cannot corrode the substantial value of our nature. "Since the intellectual nature is *creatable* only by God, and is consequently completely incorruptible with respect to the creature, to the extent that no creature can destroy it, the being who sins can therefore destroy nothing of its nature by its own act"—*Quia natura intellectualis a solo Deo est creabilis, et ex hoc simpliciter est incorruptibilis respectu creaturae ita quod nulla creatura potest eam destruerer, ergo peccans per actum suum non potest aliquid de natura sua destruere.* As as consequence of being created, of coming *immediately* from God, man has an incorruptible nature, which remains intact even in the sinner. *Naturalia manent integra* is a basic principle. Two centuries before Luther, this optimistic metaphysics was oriented in a direction completely opposed to the doctrine which, with the Reformer, would deem human nature basically depraved, truly corrupted by original sin. The force of this optimism, of this naturalism bound to the theology of Creation is found, after Scotus, in Ockham and Biel. We are, in conclusion, going to encounter the latter once more; we know that in the former the idea of the sovereign liberty of God, recognized in the radical contingency of the order of grace, coexists with the vigorous affirmation, in morality and law, of a natural order of human reason and liberty.

Our analysis returns, after considerable investigation, to its original point of departure: medieval humanism. This is not an artifice of exposition: we have only had to follow the course of history. We are now at the point of leaving the Middle Ages; the unity of Latin Christendom approaches its end. In the *Disputatio contra scholasticam theologiam* of 1517, Luther attacks—on free will and the forces of nature—Gabriel Biel, who represents scholasticism in his eyes. It is by pursuing a question of his commentary on the *Sentences* that, for the purposes of refutation, a considerable number of the theses of the *Disputatio* are posed. Behind this nominalist whom he criticizes, Martin Luther sees Duns Scotus, his master in "Pelagianism"—to quote a letter of 1516: *Cum Scoto suo, quantum pelagizet Gabriel* . . . ("How Gabriel "pelagizes" with his Duns Scotus . . ."). If, not too bewildered, a modern man seeks to find something characteristic of the mental world of the Middle Ages, a stirring of living humanity, he finds at the center, as a function of this preoccupation with the transcendent and the supernatural, a humanism embracing a naturalism that can be expressed by the Scotist formula *dignificare naturam.* But it must not be forgotten that the One who creates natures, who reveals the meaning of this Creation and effects their salvation by uniting them to Him, is the God of charity made manifest in Christ. For medieval thought, He is revealed as the Son who returns to the Father of dogmatic theology; is this fact absolutely divorced from the thought of later philosophers? This may be questioned by the historian of philosophy who knows that the interpretation of the Christian message and of the very person of Jesus presented a problem for Spinoza, Hegel, and Bergson.

BIBLIOGRAPHY

This bibliography, considerably more extensive than that of the French edition, is not meant for the specialist, who will already know where to look. Its purpose is merely to introduce the reader who may wish to pursue his interest further to some important studies of medieval thought in English. An exception to this general rule has been made so as to include some works in foreign languages that are either cited by the author or alluded to in the text. First some books on various aspects of the intellectual life of the Middle Ages in general:

Carré, M. H. *Realists and Nominalists.* London, 1946.

Crombie, A. C. *Augustine to Galileo: The History of Science A.D. 400-1650.* London, 1952.

Curtis, S. J. *A Short History of Western Philosophy in the Middle Ages.* London, 1951.

Fairweather, E. R. *A Scholastic Miscellany: Anselm to Ockham.* Philadelphia, 1956.

Geyer, B. *Die patristische und scholastische Philosophie* (Vol. 2 of *Friedrich Ueberwegs Grundriss der Geschichte der Philosophie*). Berlin, 1928.

Gilson, E. *History of Christian Philosophy in the Middle Ages.* New York, 1955.

——— *Reason and Revelation in the Middle Ages.* New York, 1938.

——— *The Spirit of Mediaeval Philosophy.* New York, 1936.

Hawkins, D. J. B. *A Sketch of Mediaeval Philosophy.* New York, 1947.

Le Goff, J. *Les intellectuels au moyen âge.* Paris, 1957.

Landgraf, A. M. *Einführung in die Geschichte der theologischen Literatur der Frühscholastik.* Regensburg, 1948.

McKeon, R. *Selections from Medieval Philosophers.* 2 vols. New York, 1929-1930.

Rashdall, H. *The Universities of Europe in the Middle Ages* (revised ed. by F. M. Powicke and Q. B. Emden). 3 vols. Oxford, 1936.

Seeberg, R. *Lehrbuch der Dogmengeschichte.* Vol. 3: *Die Dogmengeschichte des Mittelalters* (5th ed.). Graz, 1953.

Taylor, H. O. *The Mediaeval Mind* (4th ed.). 2 vols. New York, 1925.

Wulf, M. de. *History of Mediaeval Philosophy* (to be completed in 3 vols.). Vol. 1, Edinburgh, 1952.

———— *Philosophy and Civilization in the Middle Ages.* Princeton, 1922.

CHAPTER I

Bett, H. *Johannes Scotus Erigena: A Study in Mediaeval Philosophy.* Cambridge, 1925.

Burch, C. B. *Early Medieval Philosophy.* New York, 1951.

Duckett, E. S. *Alcuin, Friend of Charlemagne.* New York, 1951.

Haskins, C. H. *The Renaissance of the Twelfth Century.* New York, 1957.

Roques, R. *L'univers dionysien.* Paris, 1954.

Webb, C. C. J. *John of Salisbury.* London, 1932.

CHAPTER II

Barth, K. *Fides quaerens intellectum: Anselms Beweis der Existenz Gottes in Zusammenhang seines theologischen Programms.* Munich, 1931.

Ghellinck, J. de. *Le mouvement théologique du XIIe siècle* (2nd. ed.). Bruges, 1948.

Gilson, E. *Heloise and Abelard.* Chicago, 1951.

———— *The Mystical Theology of Saint Bernard.* New York, 1940.

McCallum, J. R. *Abailard's Ethics.* Oxford, 1935.

———— *Abelard's Christian Theology.* Oxford, 1948.

McIntyre, J. *St. Anselm and His Critics.* Edinburgh, 1954.

Stolz, A. *Anselm von Canterbury.* Munich, 1937.

Webb, C. C. J. *Studies in the History of Natural Theology.* Oxford, 1915.

Williams, W. W. *Saint Bernard of Clairvaux.* Manchester, 1935.

CHAPTER III

Chenu, M.-D. *La théologie comme science au XIIIe siècle* (3rd ed.). Paris, 1957.

Gilson, E. *Dante the Philosopher.* New York, 1949.

Husik, I. *A History of Mediaeval Jewish Philosophy.* New York, 1958.

O'Leary, D. *Arabic Thought and Its Place in History.* London, 1939.

Mandonnet, P. *Siger de Brabant et l'averroisme latin au XIIIe siècle* (2nd ed.). 2 vols. Louvain, 1908-11.

Mullally, J. P. *The Summulae logicales of Peter of Spain.* Notre Dame, Indiana, 1945.

Nardi, B. *Sigieri di Brabante nel pensiero del rinascimento italiano.* Rome, 1945.

Van Steenberghen, F. *Aristotle in the West.* Louvain, 1955.

———— *The Philosophical Movement in the Thirteenth Century.* Edinburgh, 1955.

———— *Siger de Brabant d'après ses oeuvres inédites.* 2 vols. Louvain, 1931-42.

CHAPTER IV

Bridges, J. H. *The Life and Work of Roger Bacon.* London, 1914.

Callus, D. A. *The Condemnation of Saint Thomas at Oxford.* Oxford, 1946.

———— (ed.). *Robert Grosseteste, Scholar and Bishop. Essays in Commemoration of the Seventh Centenary of His Death.* Oxford, 1955.

Chenu, M.-D. *Introduction à l'étude de saint Thomas d'Aquin.* Paris, 1950.

Copleston, F. C. *Aquinas.* London, 1955.

Crombie, A. C. *Robert Grosseteste and the Origins of Experimental Science, 1100-1700.* Oxford, 1953.

Crowley, T. *Roger Bacon: The Problem of the Soul in His Philosophical Commentaries.* Louvain, 1950.

D'Arcy, M. C. *St. Thomas Aquinas* (2nd ed.). Westminster, Maryland, 1955.

Easton, S. C. *Roger Bacon and His Search for a Universal Science.* New York, 1952.

Gilson, E. *The Christian Philosophy of St. Thomas Aquinas.* New York, 1956.

———— *The Philosophy of St. Bonaventure.* New York, 1938.

Maréchal, J. *Le point de départ de la métaphysique.* Vol. V: *Le Thomisme devant la philosophie critique.* Louvain, 1926.

Peers, E. A. *Ramon Lull.* London, 1929.

Rohmer, J. *La finalité morale chez les théologiens de saint Augustin à Duns Scot.* Paris, 1939.

Sertillanges, A. D. *Saint Thomas Aquinas and His Work.* London, 1957.

Sharp, D. E. *Franciscan Philosophy at Oxford in the Thirteenth Century.* London, 1930.

Thomson, S. H. *The Writings of Robert Grosseteste, Bishop of Lincoln, 1235-1253.* Cambridge, 1940.

CHAPTER V

Boehner, P. (ed.). *Ockham: Philosophical Writings.* Edinburgh, 1957.

Gilson, E. *Jean Duns Scot: Introduction à ses positions fondamentales.* Paris, 1952.

Harris, C. R. S. *Duns Scotus.* 2 vols. Oxford, 1927.

Lagarde, G. de. *La naissance de l'esprit laïque au décline du moyen âge.* Vols. 5 and 6: *L'individualisme ockhamiste.* Paris, 1946.

Longpré, E. *La philosophie de Duns Scot.* Paris, 1924.

Moody, E. A. *The Logic of William of Ockham.* New York, 1935.

CHAPTER VI

Bett, H. *Nicholas of Cusa.* London, 1932.

Clark, J. M. *The Great German Mystics, Eckhart, Tauler and Suso.* Oxford, 1949.

Duhem, P. *Le système du monde.* 8 vols. Paris, 1913-58.

Heron, G. (trans.). *Nicolas Cusanus, On Learned Ignorance.* New Haven, 1954.

Koyré, A. *From the Closed World to the Infinite Universe.* Baltimore, 1957.

———— "Le vide et l'espace infini au XIVe siècle," in *Archives d'histoire doctrinale et littéraire du moyen âge,* 17 (1949), 45-91.

Maier, A. *Die Vorläufer Galileis im 14. Jahrhundert: Studien zur Naturphilosophie der Spätscholastik.* Rome, 1949.

———— *Zwei Grundprobleme der scholastischen Naturphilosophie* (2nd ed.). Rome, 1951.

Muller-Thym, B. J. *The Establishment of the University of Being in the Doctrine of Meister Eckhart of Hochheim.* New York, 1939.

Volpe, G. della. *Il misticismo speculativo di Maestro Eckhart nei suoi rapporti storici.* Bologna, 1930.

Weinberg, J. R. *Nicolaus of Autrecourt: A Study in 14th Century Thought.* Princeton, 1948.

INDEX

PAUL VIGNAUX

Paul Vignaux is a leading French scholar in philosophy and theology whose PHILOSOPHY IN THE MIDDLE AGES *has also been published in Italian, Spanish, and Portuguese translations. Among his other books are* JUSTIFICATION ET PRÉDESTINATION AU XIVe SIÈCLE, LUTHER COMMENTATEUR DES SENTENCES, *and* NOMINALISME AU XIVe SIÈCLE.

E. C. Hall, the translator of this volume, is assistant professor of history at Wayne State University.